GORDON ALLPORT

The Man and His Ideas

DR. RICHARD I. EVANS is Professor of Psychology and coordinates the graduate social psychology program at the University of Houston. He received his B.S. and M.S. degrees in Psychology at the University of Pittsburgh and his Ph.D. in Psychology at Michigan State University. Under a National Science Foundation grant, he has filmed dialogues with the world's most notable psychologists, including Carl Jung, Erich Fromm, Erik Erikson, and B. F. Skinner, from which the books in this series are derived. He is a pioneer in educational television and the social psychology of communication, and taught the nation's first college course on noncommercial television. His continuing concern with sound public education in psychology has led to frequent appearances on commercial and educational television programs. He has published a number of professional articles in social psychology. His most recent books are *Resistance to Innovation in Higher Education, B. F. Skinner: The Man and His Ideas, Psychology and Arthur Miller,* and *Social Psychology in Life* (with R. M. Rozelle).

GORDON ALLPORT

RICHARD I. EVANS

The Man and His Ideas

E. P. DUTTON & CO., INC.
NEW YORK   1970

Volume VI in the series "Dialogues
with Notable Contributors
to Personality Theory"
Published simultaneously in Canada
by Clarke, Irwin & Company Limited,
Toronto and Vancouver | Library
of Congress Catalog Card Number:
74-125908
SBN 0-525-11602-8
Grateful acknowledgment is made
to the American Psychological
Association for permission to reprint
the article "Gordon Willard Allport,
1897–1967" by Thomas F. Pettigrew,
which first appeared in the *Journal
of Personality and Social Psychology,*
Vol. 12, No. 1.

First Edition

To
my lovely wife and children

ACKNOWLEDGMENTS

In the long process involved in filming and taping the dialogues with Gordon W. Allport and transcribing, editing, and integrating them into the present volume, I am indebted to a great many individuals. Though space prohibits mentioning everyone who so kindly assisted in this venture, I wish to express my appreciation to at least some of them.

During the early stages of preparation of the manuscript, psychology graduate student Judith Woodard gave editorial assistance which is significantly reflected in this volume. For her efforts I am most appreciative.

Grateful acknowledgment is made to the University of Houston for permission to utilize the printed texts of the filmed and taped dialogue. Mr. James Bauer of the University of Houston, who functioned in the demanding role of technical director for the taping and filming sessions, should also be mentioned among those who have greatly assisted me.

I wish to express my thanks to my secretary, Miss Miriam Thompson, who with great patience and care handled the demanding chore of collating, rechecking, and typing the final form of the manuscript.

I am grateful for the support from the National Science Foundation, without which this project could not have been implemented.

Thanks are accorded to Dr. Thomas F. Pettigrew of Harvard University for allowing us to edit slightly and use as an introduction to the present volume his fine tribute to Professor Allport which appeared first in the *Journal of Personality and Social Psychology.* In fact, Dr. Pettigrew's involvement in this volume from the beginning and his willingness to communicate on our behalf with Mrs. Gordon W. Allport is much appreciated. Mrs. Allport's interest is particularly important to us and is most gratifying.

I appreciate the kindness of the three symposium participants (all distinguished students of Dr. Allport), Dr. Pettigrew, Dr. M. Brewster Smith of the University of California, and Dr. John Harding of Cornell University, not only for their willingness to allow us to include the transcript of the American Psychological Association symposium, "Gordon Allport: His Unique Contributions to Contemporary Personality and Social Psychology" as part of the present volume, but for editing the transcript where necessary in the service of accuracy.

Finally, the wonderful cooperation of the late Professor Gordon W. Allport cannot be emphasized enough. Not only was he willing to participate in the filming and audio-taping sessions which were involved in this project, but his genuine good humor during the course of what was surely an unfamiliar role for him, along with his thoughtful reactions after viewing the filmed portion of these dialogues, will long be remembered by us all.

RICHARD I. EVANS
Professor of Psychology
University of Houston

CONTENTS

INTRODUCTION

Gordon W. Allport was born in 1897 in Indiana and grew up in Cleveland, the son of a physician, in a home characterized by "plain Protestant piety and hard work [Allport, 1967]." His long involvement with Harvard University began in 1915 when his brother, Floyd, encouraged him to apply. In those more leisurely days, he decided during the summer to enroll and arrived in September to take his entrance examinations. From this almost casual acceptance, his deep devotion to his alma mater never waned: "In the course of fifty years' association with Harvard I have never ceased to admire the unspoken expectation of excellence [Allport, 1967]."

Allport's career was characterized by a convergence of interest in both personality and social psychology, in science and social issues, in psychology and social ethics. His undergraduate years foretold this convergence. He was impressed by his first teacher in psychology, Münsterberg ("looking like Wotan"), and wondered if Münsterberg's total separation of "causal from purposive" psychology might "not be reconciled and fused." He concentrated in both psychology and social ethics. And he spent much of his spare time in social service: conducting a boys' club in Boston's West End, visiting for the Family Society, serving as a volunteer probation officer, registering homes for war workers, and assisting foreign students.

Upon graduation in 1919, Allport seized the opportunity to be an early version of a Peace Corpsman. He taught English and Sociology at Robert College in Constantinople, and made such a lasting impression upon his students that they surprised him with a reunion party in Athens thirty-six years later.

Returning to Harvard in 1920, he took his Ph.D. in psychology two years later. His dissertation title illustrated once again the pull between science and social concern: *An Experimental Study of the Traits of Personality: With Special Reference to the Problem of Social Diagnosis*. Awarded a coveted Sheldon Travelling Fellowship, Allport studied for two years abroad—"a second intellectual dawn" he later described them. He spent the first year primarily in Germany, where he was particularly attracted to the new Gestalt school. He spent the second year at Cambridge, where his reports on Gestalt developments were coolly received by the British psychologists of the day. On his return to the United States, he married Ada Lufkin Gould, a clinical psychologist herself, who loyally supported him in his work. Their son, Robert, in now a pediatrician in Maine.

In 1924 Allport became a Harvard instructor in social ethics. Two years later he temporarily severed his connection with his university to accept an assistant professorship in psychology at Dartmouth. But even during these brief four years at Hanover he repeatedly returned to Harvard to teach in summer school. In 1930 he came to Cambridge to stay. His contributions to Harvard were many. In 1924 and 1925 he taught what is thought to be the first course on personality offered in an American college. In the late forties he taught the introductory course for the new Social Relations Department and, despite high standards, fashioned it into the most popular course in the college. An early advocate of interdisciplinary perspectives, he actively participated in the faculty committee which established the university's Sociology Department in 1931. And he was especially proud of his role in helping to found the Department of Social Relations in 1946, a department which uniquely combines degree programs in clinical psychology, social anthropology, social psychology, and sociology. Over 300 Ph.D.s remember Allport best for his service to the Department for eighteen long years as the warm but rigorous chairman of the Committee on Higher Degrees. "He knew all the rules," admired one graduate student, "but he never internalized them."

Allport's worldwide fame, of course, rested chiefly upon his innovative contributions to the psychology of personality. In 1937 he published the first comprehensive statement of his position, *Personality: A Psychological Interpretation* (Allport, 1937), now a widely cited classic. He refined his position further in *Becoming: Basic Considerations for a Psychology of Personality* (Allport, 1955) and *Pattern and Growth in Personality* (Allport, 1961). Three collections of papers, culled from among his over 160 published pieces, have appeared: *The Nature of Personality: Selected Papers* (Allport, 1950b), *Personality and Social Encounter* (Allport, 1960b), and *The Person in Psychology: Selected Essays* (Allport, 1968). All told, he produced a dozen books and a pair of monographs; eighteen foreign editions of these volumes have been published in ten languages ranging from Greek and Norwegian to Japanese and Korean.

Allport tenaciously sought a "full-bodied psychology" of the individual human being. His thesis research began his quest for an appropriate unit of personality which culminated in his conception of the "trait"; his concern with the problem of the developmental transformation that motives undergo culminated in his distinctive concept of "functional autonomy"; his interest in intentionality culminated in his emphasis upon "propriate" functions. Allport's theory stresses unique individuality, human maturity, and conscious forces. He made less of unconscious forces than most personality theorists in large part, perhaps, because his own self-knowledge was so complete. This led him, too, to a position on personal assessment, which also raised eyebrows when it bluntly appeared in *The Use of Personal Documents in Psychological Science* (Allport, 1942). In an age of indirection, Allport insisted, "If you want to know something about a person, why not first ask him?" Eventually his position helped right the balance in assessment (see especially Allport, 1953), but it was considered scandalously naive when he introduced it.

An eclectic, open-system theorist, Allport has been simultaneously criticized for the loose structure of his theory and such explicit statements as his position on assessment. Part of this double-barreled complaint stems from his vivid writing style. Hall and Lindzey (1957, pp. 258–259), in their perceptive chapter on Allport, put the matter well:

Against the background of these many years of college teaching, it should come as no surprise that in much of his professional writing Allport displays a deliberate didactic intent. In contrast to most technical writers, whose primary goal appears to be the construction of irreproachable statements that defy the efforts of the critic to find a tooth-hold, Allport seems much more interested in expressing issues in a salient, provocative fashion. This sometimes leads to overstatement or else to focusing upon a particular issue to the relative exclusion of other pertinent questions. Thus, it might be said that Allport is one of the most hotly criticized of psychological theorists, but in the same breath it should be mentioned that questions Allport has raised have usually become matters of general concern to psychologists.

He could never be accused, however, of not being open to new research findings, to new insights and experiences. A modest, thoughtful man, he was the antithesis of the rigid, dogmatic theorist. In fact, much of his time and energy went into research, where he characteristically adopted a great variety of methods: the development of two widely employed "nomothetic" tests of personality (Allport & Allport, 1949; Allport, Vernon, & Lindzey, 1960); the application of ingenious laboratory procedures to the study of expressive movement (Allport & Vernon, 1933) and radio response (Allport & Cantril, 1935); and one of the most fascinating case histories in the psychological literature, *Letters from Jenny* (Allport, 1965). From his early Gestalt influence, he maintained a lively research interest in cognition: his studies in this area range from work on eidetic imagery (Allport, 1924; 1928) to the trapezoidal window illusion (Allport & Pettigrew, 1957) and binocular rivalry (Pettigrew, Allport, & Barnett, 1958).

Allport's work in social psychology came to rival for attention his work in personality. A chapter in Murchison's original *A Handbook of Social Psychology* fashioned the modern conception of "attitude" (Allport, 1935); and another chapter in Lindzey's *Handbook of Social Psychology* provided historical perspective on the growing discipline (Allport, 1954a). His social interests expressed themselves in his contributions to such phenomena as rumor, religious beliefs, and intergroup prejudice, as represented in his volumes on *The Psychology of Rumor* (Allport & Postman, 1947), *The Individual and His Religion* (Allport, 1950a), and *The Nature of Prejudice* (Allport, 1954b). His early paper on "Some Roots of Prejudice" (Allport

& Kramer, 1946) foretold the major directions of the later volume on the *Authoritarian Personality* (Adorno, Frenkel-Brunswik, Levinson, & Sanford, 1950). He quietly engaged, too, in activities reminiscent of his undergraduate activities in social service, from aiding refugee psychologists to escape Hitler Germany and directing the philanthropic Ella Lyman Cabot Trust, to serving on national commissions concerned with racial justice and lecturing on prejudice to the Boston police (Allport, 1945).

Often in the midst of countertrends, Allport, then, serenely pursued his own path, his own conception of a meaningful psychology. To many in the profession he has alternately appeared as old-fashioned or radical, archaic or long before his time. But his vision of a "full-bodied psychology" of the individual came increasingly into view, and he lived to see much of psychology follow the directions in which he had pioneered. By the 1950s, practicing clinical psychologists reported that they found his work second only to Freud's in day-to-day usefulness (Schafer, Berg, and McCandless, 1951). "What does a critic do," wryly asked Allport, "when his field comes to agree with him?"

His professional honors were many. In addition to the editorship of the *Journal of Abnormal and Social Psychology*, he served as president of both the American Psychological Association (1939) and the Society for the Psychological Study of Social Issues (1944), received the Gold Medal of the American Psychological Foundation (1963), held honorary fellowship status in numerous international psychological organizations,

and gave, among many famous-named lectures, the
Lowell Lectures in Boston, the Terry Lectures at Yale,
and the Hoernlé Lecture in South Africa.

Yet he resisted a "school" of followers. True to his
character as well as his doctrine of the uniqueness
of each human personality, Allport guided his students in their own, not his, direction. Though each
may show a trace of Allportian influence in his work,
his doctoral students have ranged all over the psychological map. Consider, for example, the varied
interests and contributions of John and Jean Arsenian,
Alfred Baldwin, Raymond Bauer, Jerome Bruner,
Hadley Cantril, George Coelho, Leonard Doob, John
Harding, Robert Knapp, Sheldon Korchin, Bernard
Kramer, Bernard Kutner, Lewis Long, Gardner
Lindzey, Donald McGranahan, Betty Mawardi, Henry
Odbert, Thomas Pettigrew, Leo Postman, Henry
Riecken, Fillmore Sanford, Brewster Smith, Renato
Tagiuri, Philip Vernon, and Lauren Wispe. But each
received an initial training such as few graduate
students enjoy. And, as Jerome Bruner has remarked,
"Having been a student of Gordon Allport's was a life
long connection—with Ada as well as Gordon." In
1963, fifty-five of his Ph.D.s surprised him with a
testimonial gathering and presented him with two
bound volumes of their own writings with the dedi-
cation: "From his students—in appreciation of his
respect for their individuality." "This is an intimate
honor," he confessed, "and one I prize above all
others."

As a young science, American psychology has not
yet had many men whose renown exceed the confines

of the discipline. But Gordon Allport was such a man to whom the profession can point with pride. For his professional colleagues, he widened the perceived alternatives open to the field. For the public, he made psychology applicable to the problems of his time and understandable to millions through his books and lectures. He was recognized in his lifetime as a great psychologist, and will certainly be so remembered.

Allport's final year at Harvard recalled his first appointment as an instructor in social ethics. In 1966 he was appointed the first Richard Clarke Cabot Professor of Social Ethics. "Since Dr. Cabot was my first 'boss' at Harvard, having much influence upon my career first and last," he wrote at the close of his life, "the appointment seemed to me to complete fittingly an intellectual cycle as well as a cycle of sentiment [Allport, 1967]." To those fortunate enough to have had this remarkable man for a teacher and colleague, Allport's death in October 1967 seems less to complete a cycle than to end an era.

REFERENCES

Adorno, T. W., Frenkel-Brunswik, E., Levinson, D. J., and Sanford, R. N. *The Authoritarian Personality.* New York: Harper, 1950.

Allport, G. W. "Eidetic imagery." *British Journal of Psychology,* 1924, 15, 99–120.

Allport, G. W. "The Eidetic Image and the Afterimage." *American Journal of Psychology,* 1928, 40, 418–425.

Allport, G. W. "Attitudes," in C. C. Murchison (ed.), *A Handbook of Social Psychology.* Worcester, Mass.: Clark University Press, 1935.

Allport, G. W. *Personality: A Psychological Interpretation.* New York: Holt, 1937.

Allport, G. W. *The Use of Personal Documents in Psychological*

Science. New York: Social Science Research Council, 1942, Bulletin 49.

Allport, G. W. "Catharsis and the Reduction of Prejudice." *Journal of Social Issues,* 1945, 1, 1–8.

Allport, G. W. *The Individual and His Religion.* New York: Macmillan, 1950. (a)

Allport, G. W. *The Nature of Personality: Selected Papers.* Reading, Mass.: Addison-Wesley, 1950. (b)

Allport, G. W. "The Trend in Motivational Theory." *American Journal of Orthopsychiatry,* 1953, 25, 107–119.

Allport, G. W. "The Historical Background of Modern Social Psychology," in G. Lindzey (ed.), *Handbook of Social Psychology.* Cambridge, Mass.: Addison-Wesley, 1954. (a)

Allport, G. W. *The Nature of Prejudice.* Reading, Mass.: Addison-Wesley, 1954. (b)

Allport, G. W. *Becoming: Basic Considerations for a Psychology of Personality.* New Haven, Conn.: Yale University Press, 1955.

Allport, G. W. "The Open System in Personality Theory. *Journal of Abnormal and Social Psychology,* 1960, 61, 301–310. (a)

Allport, G. W. *Personality and Social Encounter.* Boston: Beacon Press, 1960. (b)

Allport, G. W. *Pattern and Growth in Personality.* New York: Holt, Rinehart & Winston, 1961.

Allport, G. W. *Letters from Jenny.* New York: Harcourt, Brace & World, 1965.

Allport, G. W. "Gordon W. Allport," in E. G. Boring & G. Lindzey (eds.), *A History of Psychology in Autobiography,* Vol. 5. New York: Appleton-Century-Crofts, 1967.

Allport, G. W. *The Person in Psychology: Selected Essays.* Boston: Beacon Press, 1968.

Allport, G. W. and Allport, F. H. *A-S Reaction Study* (rev. ed.). Boston: Houghton Mifflin, 1949.

Allport, G. W. and Cantril, H. *The Psychology of Radio.* New York: Harper, 1935.

Allport, G. W. and Kramer, B. M. "Some Roots of Prejudice." *Journal of Psychology,* 1946, 22, 9–39.

Allport, G. W. and Pettigrew, T. F. "Cultural Influence on the Perception of Movement: The Trapezoidal Illusion Among

Zulus." *Journal of Abnormal and Social Psychology*, 1957, 55, 104–113.

Allport, G. W. and Postman, L. *The Psychology of Rumor*. New York: Holt, 1947.

Allport, G. W. and Vernon, P. E. *Studies in Expressive Movement*. New York: Macmillan, 1933.

Allport, G. W., Vernon, P. E., and Lindzey, G. *A Study of Values* (3d ed.). Boston: Houghton Mifflin, 1960.

Hall, C. S. and Lindzey, G. *Theories of Personality*. New York: Wiley, 1957.

Pettigrew, T. F., Allport, G. W., and Barnett, E. O. "Binocular Resolution and Perception of Race in South Africa." *British Journal of Psychology*, 1958, 49, 265–278.

Schafer, R., Berg, I., and McCandless, B. "Report on Survey of Current Psychological Testing Practices." Supplement to Newsletter, Division of Clinical and Abnormal Psychology, American Psychological Association, 1951, 4, No. 5.

THOMAS F. PETTIGREW
Harvard University

GORDON ALLPORT

The Man and His Ideas

PSYCHOANALYSIS; STIMULUS-RESPONSE THEORY; EARLY INFLUENCES

First Encounter with Freud

Freudian Repetition Compulsion

Character Typologies of
   Freud and Jung

The Unconscious

Reactions to Lewin and Eysenck

Stimulus-Response Versus More
   Individual-Centered
   Psychology

Influence of Münsterberg,
   William James, Spranger,
   and Eclecticism

PART I

Overview | In this section I endeavor to give Dr. Allport an opportunity to discuss some general background against which his theory developed. As an effective but not necessarily harsh critic of Freud and his theories, Dr. Allport responds to my questions concerning Sigmund Freud, both about his experience with him personally and on such basic Freudian notions as the repetition compulsion and the unconscious. In his responses much is revealed concerning Allport's own unique approach to the study of human personality. More insight concerning the source of Allport's orientation is apparent as we discuss his reactions to the personality type theories of Freud and Jung, and his feelings concerning whether or not the psychologist should stress stimulus-response in fairly mechanical terms or should stress the individual organism whose presence we infer between that stimulus and response. He also reacts to my questions concerning the role of free will versus determinism. His views of Hugo Münsterberg, Eduard Spranger, Kurt Lewin, and Hans Eysenck, and his interpretation of the meaning of eclecticism in psychology provide valuable background concerning Allport's theory.

EVANS: Dr. Allport, it's quite interesting and intriguing for me to visit with you here in Emerson Hall on the Harvard University campus where the history of psychology has seen such important events transpire. It was particularly interesting to see some of the places where you and Professor Münsterberg worked, and it is most appropriate that we should be talking here about some of your unique contributions to personality theory and to psychology in general.

Since most of our students begin the study of psychology by reading Freud, it might be profitable to begin by hearing your reaction to some of Freud's ideas and work. I understand you actually met Freud on one occasion, and I wonder if you would tell about this meeting.

ALLPORT: My one encounter with Freud did not turn out to be very significant for my professional development, but I'll tell the story briefly. Not long after I finished college, I found myself in Vienna where Freud was not as renowned as he became later. At any rate, I wrote him a note announcing that I was in Vienna, and that he no doubt would be glad to know it. He was very courteous and sent me a hand-written note inviting me to his office at a stated time. So I went to the famous Burggasser office which was papered in red burlap and decorated with pictures of dreams. At exactly the appointed time, Freud opened the door of his inner office, invited me in smilingly, sat down, and said nothing. It suddenly occurred to me that it was up to me to have a reason for calling on him, but actually I didn't have any. I was just curious. I fished around in my mind and came up with an event which occurred on the tramcar on the way to his office that I thought would interest him. There had been a little boy about four years old who obviously had already developed a dirt phobia. His mother was a *Hausfrau*, well starched and very prim, and the little boy would say he didn't want to sit there; it was dirty. He didn't want that man to sit next to him; he was dirty. And so it went throughout the whole trip. I thought this might interest Freud since the phobia seemed to be set so early in this case. He listened till I finished; then he fixed his very therapeutic eyes on me and said, "and was that little boy you?" It honestly was not, but I felt guilty. At any rate, I managed to change the conversation. In thinking over the experience, it impressed me that Freud's tendency was to see pathological trends, and since most of the people who came to see him were patients, it was natural that he'd think I was a patient and break down my defenses in order to get on with the business. Actually, he mistook my motives in this case. Had he said to himself that I was a brassy American youth imposing on his good nature and time, he would have been fairly correct. But to ascribe my motivation to unconscious motives as he did in this case was definitely wrong. As I thought over the experience in subsequent years, it occurred to me that there might be a place for another type of theory to account for personality and motivation.

EVANS: It's interesting that your one experience with Freud had this impact on you. Freud's own model of personality was a kind of recapitulation model of behavior which postulates that the very early levels of development fairly well mold the individual for the rest of his life. This is illustrated by the young man who looks for a mother in his wife, and the young woman who looks for a father figure to marry, and so on. Freud felt people were more or less trapped by these early patterns and tended to be governed by them continuously, even though they might be unconsciously operating. Do you feel this notion—the so-called repetition compulsion—is relevant beyond the application to psychoanalytic practice?

ALLPORT: It would seem that this formula of Freud's fits some neurotic lives pretty well because they are seeking infantile satisfactions, or repeating regardless of appropriateness certain infantile patterns. However, I don't believe that this concept applies at all to normal personality development. We are obviously not finished developing by the age of five, and many people show entirely contrary tendencies. But I would agree that this formula would be adequate to describe a good many neuroses which were discovered to be of the infantile type.

EVANS: How do you feel about Freud's notion that the child comes into the world a very dependent organism dedicated to the satisfaction of its own needs, and that only through experience and growth can it learn to direct these needs away from itself?

ALLPORT: I think the infant, or the child of two, is astonishingly self-centered. It has to be; it's the nature of the organism. Just imagine what would happen if a person of twenty showed the thoughtlessness, the grabbiness, the immediacy of gratification, and self-centeredness that the two year old shows. It would be incredible. I think that the origin of life is hedonistic, or self-centered, if you wish, but a change occurs which makes a person much more aware of others, and extends his sense of selfhood gradually, perhaps to the end of his life.

EVANS: Freud contended, however, that both the pathological and the normal person may have fixations to some degree at this early level and may never be able to grow away from the self-centeredness characteristic of the early age.

ALLPORT: Of course, we're all of us self-centered to a certain degree, but just because we are self-centered doesn't inevitably mean that self-centeredness must dominate our natures. There may be traces of infantilism in all of us, but there are more mature ways of being egotistical and self-seeking. We're constantly in conflict about this, but my point is that some people become socialized, and their ego is so extended that a true altruistic tendency can be the dominant feature of their personality.

EVANS: Dr. Allport, how might you react to the notion of character typologies such as Freud postulated as, for instance, the oral type which he felt evolved out of the infant's sucking reflex involving a fixation at the "oral level" of development, leading to an individual who is passive and dependent?

ALLPORT: Freud's notion that fixation at some level of psychosexual development leads to certain character types has never appealed to me very much. In fact, I don't know very much evidence in that favor. To make typological categories is, in my mind, a very dangerous and arbitrary approach. I would suspect that once in a hundred cases you might find a person who just fitted a classical Freudian oral type or anal type, and for this person, the label might be useful. I don't believe that the typologies represent measurable qualities; they are not fixed qualities, and I've never found them too useful.

EVANS: What you're suggesting, then, is that the whole idea of typologies might present some limitations, whether you use Freud's, Jung's, or Rank's categories. In fact, was this not the point at which your thinking departed from the trend in psychology toward typologies and led you to begin to look for a more meaningful theory of personality?

ALLPORT: There are types and there are types, but none of them has ever suited me. The best conception, I feel, is a concept of ideal types which doesn't pretend to incorporate any given personality entirely. The difficulty with any typology is that it slices out of the individual certain qualities which are like certain qualities in another individual, and that makes a type—extraverted, oral, etc. But the type never includes the entire personality because the extraversion in one person is related more to his own intelligence, submission, leadership, and anxiety than it is to extraversion per se in another person. A trait must be related to the pattern of the personality of which it is a part. I sort of have a feeling that we're slicing off half the personality and putting it into a type, and losing the integration of those typological characteristics with the rest of the personality. I'd rather focus on the whole person than on a somewhat abstracted type.

EVANS: By way of making some defense of typology here, may I inject that in my encounter with Carl Jung (12), he remarked that he was rather upset by the fact that American psychologists had used his introversion-extraversion typologies as a kind of whipping boy in their eagerness to discredit all type theories of personality. Jung felt that his typologies were intended to be no more than a frame of reference useful in the beginning of a therapeutic relationship. He did not intend to categorize the person into *either* extravert or introvert categories as some American psychologists accused him of doing. Would you even question the use of typologies in the manner in which Jung intended?

ALLPORT: Not exactly. I would defend Jung, I believe, because I think he meant what he said, namely, that these are important dimensions. If you want to compare people on dimensions, I'm all for that, but you mustn't confuse the fact that you're studying individual comparisons on dimensions with the totality of the individual personality. I think Jung's contribution to those dimensions—extraversion, introversion, sensation, intuitive, thinking, feeling subtypes, etc.—constitutes a very valuable addition. I regard his categories as useful, common traits by which to compare people, and I suspect that's what Jung meant. He didn't want to categorize people completely into eight tight types or permutations.

EVANS: The notion of typology seems to keep emerging in the history of psychology as a kind of easy solution to the question of personality description. Professor Kurt Lewin (17), discussing differences between Galileian and Aristotelian modes of thought, once spoke of the problem of labeling, saying that once a label has been applied, we forget it is merely a label and try to explain the group in terms of the label. I wonder how frequently we continue to fall into the same trap.

ALLPORT: Lewin, of course, would have nothing to do with types because he felt the field to be so fluid, where everything is related to many variables in a situation. As you suggest, he certainly wouldn't stick labels on persons permanently, and I think he's right in that respect. At the same time, we've got to have some tools of analysis. Someone said once that the only thing you can do about total personality is to send flowers to it. One must have some sort of dimensions or conceptual schemata in order to get hold of personality, and I feel that the doctrine of common traits is consistent with the classical idea of individual differences. You can measure degrees of extraversion or introversion or anxiety or dominance, and what not, and I think that has a very real comparative differential value in the study of personality. But the final requirement, and that which it does not do, is to put these bits and pieces into unity with the person himself. For example, my lung has more to do with my heart than it does with your lung, but a comparative analysis of lungs would cut across people and tell us nothing about the pattern within the person.

EVANS: Of course, Hans Eysenck in London has resurrected the typology notion by saying that it is a valid orientation with which to study behavior, and we should not ignore it. How 'do you feel about this, Dr. Allport?

ALLPORT: I'm in favor of Eysenck's work; it's empirical in that he doesn't just dream up type categories as many investigators have done. But it is subject to the same limitations I spoke of before. He takes common traits such as degrees of anxiety, tendencies toward neurotic behavior, radicalism, and conservatism, and by factor analysis he finds that you can isolate one or two important dimensions which cover quite a lot of the person's behavior. For certain practical purposes, that's good enough. But I come back to my main criticism, that it doesn't deal with the internal patterning of the individual which is the neuropsychic structure that nature gives us. So, I would say that Eysenck still doesn't go far enough, even though his is an empirical typology made up of common traits. It does involve research, and for that reason it's good so far as it goes.

EVANS: Referring back for a moment to your experience with Freud where you emphasized that his stress on unconscious motivation leads to the question of the role of the unconscious versus conscious in a theory of personality, we might ask how "consciousness oriented" should a psychology of personality be.

ALLPORT: I suppose on the whole I would place more weight on ego or consciousness than Freud would do, yet I can't deny the existence of repressed traces. I think that I would relate repressed traces to a neurotic disposition or a somewhat dissociated type of person. For example, let's take two individuals. In one you explore his unconscious through projective methods or through psychoanalysis, and you find that he has a great deal of anxiety. But consciously, he may deny it; he says he is a very composed person. In the second person you find the same amount of anxiety, but consciously he says, "I know that I am anxious . . . I told you that all along." It would seem that the critical factor here is whether the conscious and the unconscious measures agree, and if they agree, then you don't need the unconscious measures. You can just ask the person, and he says he's an anxious person, and he's right. You must distinguish between what he knows about himself and what he doesn't know about himself. Contrary to Freud, I suspect that most of our conflicts are very conscious; we are quite aware of them, as well as the forces acting on us. I can't deny that there may be repressed traces in some personalities, maybe a small amount in many, but the dominant motivation and conflict, I feel, are at the conscious level.

EVANS: Some of the more orthodox Freudians might react to your statement by raising the issue of what Freud referred to as overdeterminism. For example, the Freudians might point out that the evidence Freud presented in *Psychopathology of Everyday Life* (14) indicates that anything we do could be interpreted in terms of underlying unconscious motivation. Perhaps what you're saying here is that the unconscious might have some valid meaning for the diagnosis of pathology, but that for the normal individual such a theory of unconscious determinism is not particularly relevant.

ALLPORT: Insofar as being suspicious that there's an overemphasis on the unconscious determinism of everything one does, I can only refer again to my visit with Freud. He read too much into it by ascribing my motives to unconscious forces.

EVANS: Speaking of this tendency to overexplain behavior such as you have related about Freud, do you sometimes find that colleagues and students tend to do just that after they have been exposed to even a little bit of what Freud wrote?

ALLPORT: Students often become overenthusiastic; it's their religion; it's the ultimate truth, and so on. But I find that they generally outgrow it as far as they should, because there is a residual value in Freudian contributions. It seems to be a natural part of the maturing process to have one enthusiasm and then another, so I don't hold it against my students when they interpret everything I say in Freudian terms. And likewise, I don't hold it against my colleagues when they do it, because it takes all types.

EVANS: Dr. Allport, your writing and thinking has transversed an important shift in theoretical orientation in psychology, where the stimulus-response (SR) paradigm which de-emphasizes the organism has been increasingly challenged by the stimulus-organism-response (SOR) paradigm which attributes more importance to the organism and its characteristics. Though both of these two points of view are still operant in our theoretical outlook today, they present two diverging streams of thought which would seem to present a particularly difficult problem for the young student entering psychology. Do you feel that it would be possible for the young scholar to accept the validity of both points of view and still make some sense out of psychology?

ALLPORT: I think that he should first of all realize that the simple SR model is extremely attractive because it is based on a very healthy desire to know exactly what is going on, and both stimuli and responses can be measured quite accurately. It presents an objective model on which to base psychological theory, which is a very attractive notion. I'm quite well aware of its attractiveness, as I was trained mostly by behaviorists. On the other hand, it seems to me that with some nine trillion brain cells, what's going on inside the organism simply cannot be adequately depicted in terms of SR. This suggests that the variable organism, or "O," might come into basic psychological science as a necessary middle term. It's often called an intervening variable, and I feel that it is not only necessary, but needs to be a very, very large "O." I would argue for a small "s" and a small "r," but a very large "O," because it seems to me that all the interesting things in personality lie in the inferences we must make about what's going on in these intervening variables in terms of motivation, interests, attitudes, values, and so on. On the other hand, I may add one warning about the nature of "O." You could also consider the "O" as a being trying to establish an equilibrium of contradictory forces impinging on itself, and that "O" represents this homeostatic mechanism at work.

EVANS: You're using homeostasis as the biologist does, in the sense that he postulates that the organism seeks a physiological balance regardless of how much imbalance there is, are you not?

ALLPORT: Yes, that's exactly what I mean. If you consider the O as having tension-reducing propensities, or as establishing homeostasis or equilibrium, that is one view of O. Actually, however, I take a more proactive view of the nature of O. As I see it, it not only tries to establish equilibrium under some circumstances, but also attempts to maintain disequilibrium. It even goes out to seek disequilibrium in order to maintain tension. So your conception of the nature of the O forms the basis for your notion of what personality really is.

EVANS: As we probe further into the implications of the O in the model, does this not also embrace the notion of personal responsibility or self-determinism? For example, we can see that there has been a change in the concept of responsibility since Freud's introduction of a biological-unconscious determinism to the notion of environmental-social determinism emphasized by the behaviorists and sociologists, and now that the O takes on more importance in the model, we see the notion of self-determinism becoming more important. So we might ask how much emphasis should the organism be given in the self-deterministic model of human behavior?

ALLPORT: You have leapt into the most difficult question of all—the problem that the philosophers call human freedom. I think I would answer simply that we have a great many processes possible, such as intention, planning, setting of goals far off into the future, what William James called the power of keeping the selective idea uppermost. No one can answer the question of freedom in terms of yes or no. Speaking as a psychologist and a scientist, I have to say that I think man has a great deal more freedom than he ever uses, simply because he operates out of habits, prejudices, and stereotypes, often going off, as it were, half-cocked. If he reflected and kept uppermost the selective set to ask himself, "Is this my style of life or isn't it?" he would have a lot more self-determinism than is reflected in the traditional materialistic, mechanistic view of man as a reactive being. Of course, our behavior is to some extent determined by society, heredity, and our organic nature, and we must acknowledge that; but beyond that it revolves around whether we consider O a proactive or just a reactive organism. I am inclined to think that the answer lies in the direction of proaction, thereby admitting into psychology the importance of such concepts as goals, purposes, intentions, plans, values, and the like. I would say that we have more freedom than most of today's psychology admits. I would not, however, argue for the absolute untrammeled freedom espoused by some of the existentialists. The answer lies somewhere in the middle course.

EVANS: We sometimes see that as laymen become more familiar with psychological concepts they tend to popularize them and often use them incorrectly. To illustrate this, overstated theories of social determinism have changed attitudes toward juvenile delinquents from "punishing the delinquent" to holding "society" responsible for the delinquent's behavior. The whole notion of social determinism as against self-responsibility provides a rationalization for the delinquent. He's not responsible for his acts. He places the blame on some indefinite "they" representing society. In fact, in that song about Officer Krupke in the musical, *West Side Story*, the delinquents sarcastically sing about not being responsible for their problems—society is.

ALLPORT: Again, it seems to me that truth lies somewhere in the middle course. We should be aware of the parent-child relationship and of the antecedent parental behavior that engenders certain responses in the child. In the area of delinquency, it is important to recognize that neighborhood gangs, mass media, and the like do have predisposing influences. At the same time, I don't see why in the field of "character education" we shouldn't put more responsibility on the child at an early age and attempt to help him internalize some set of norms and values that will eventually be meaningful for him. I would never remove from the child a certain sense of responsibility. One of the problems in our American democracy is that the youth have a firm notion of their rights to life, liberty, and the pursuit of happiness without a counterbalancing emphasis on the reciprocal duties that are also a part of life. We've been a little short teaching them that there are no rights in life without duties.

EVANS: Incidentally, since we've been speaking of early influences on the individual in the abstract, it might be interesting to get a bit more personal here, and ask you to identify some of the individuals who influenced *you* most in your own early training.

ALLPORT: My first teacher in psychology was Hugo Münsterberg at Harvard. He was such a bad teacher, in the traditional sense, that he intrigued me and I decided to go into psychology to find out what he was talking about. Since then I have never known what a good teacher or bad teacher really was because his influence was so great. He lectured with a heavy German accent and his text was often not too clear. I had some behavioristically inclined teachers, such as E. B. Holt and H. S. Langfeld, who almost persuaded me while I was a student. But after receiving the Ph.D., I went to Germany where I encountered the Gestalt movement. It hadn't been known in this country at all before then. The concept of dynamical self-distribution of the brain field seemed to me to be rather important in that it postulated something going on within the organism which was unique to the organism. William Stern, who invented the I.Q. concept, had a personalistic psychology that evolved into the tradition of studying individual differences. He was also a critic of the tradition, holding that the patterning of the person must be taken into account, not just the separate traits. I studied with him for a semester in Hamburg, and he had a great deal of influence on me. The net effect of my study in Europe was that by the time I returned to America I was already a little bit out of touch and out of step with the Anglo-American traditions of positivism, statistics, and objectivism. Ever since then I've been somewhat of a maverick. William James's writings have made me perhaps less patient with the strict SR system because it represents a narrow type of psychological system. One of my German teachers, Eduard Spranger, was the source for the Study of Values test that I devised in the American vein. The test was American, but the idea that there are six fundamental types of values or evaluations that man may hold or make was German. These are perhaps my most influential teachers, but I have found a great deal of congeniality among my colleagues such as Rogers, Gardner Murphy, Kurt Lewin, and Professor Henry Murray. I always felt they were supporting whatever line of development my thinking took. I would call them first cousins of my thinking.

EVANS: Even this brief background suggests that your position is one which has encompassed many theoretical positions in psychology, such as behaviorism, psychonanalysis, personalistic psychology, and field theory, and your theory of personality integrates many aspects of these systems. It leads me to ask here, Dr. Allport, how you feel about the label of eclecticism since in a sense you are an eclectic. This is a position often termed a weak one, but you have written in defense of eclecticism. On what grounds do you defend it?

ALLPORT: Let's distinguish first two kinds of eclecticism. I draw my distinction from the German poet Goethe, who differentiated between jackdaw eclecticism and systematic eclecticism. Jackdaw eclecticism is where you bring everything to the nest regardless of what it is, and systematic eclecticism is where you try to make one unified whole out of all of your borrowings. I suppose in a sense I am eclectic; for one thing, I am historically oriented in that I am an academic psychologist, and I think I have drawn from the history of psychology what I find necessary and meaningful.

SOME UNIQUE CONTRIBUTIONS

PART II

Overview | In this section I endeavor to provide Dr. Allport with an opportunity to discuss some of his unique contributions to personality psychology. Here he discusses his penetrating analysis of the personality trait, analyzing, for example, his distinction between common and unique traits, and the entire problem of the nomothetic versus the idiographic orientation to the study of personality. We also discuss his now classic but controversial notion of functional autonomy of motives, which challenges all the traditional historical approaches to the understanding of human motivation, such as Freud's. We conclude this section by discussing his particular approach to the understanding of the self, self-awareness, and how his notion of the proprium is relevant in this understanding.

EVANS: Dr. Allport, you have, of course, been identified with the personality trait and the way in which it can be used in assessing personality. It would be very interesting to know a little more about how you happened to develop this focus and how you feel about the label "trait psychologist" which some psychologists have given you.

ALLPORT: When I was a student just beginning to be interested in differential psychology, this field was most clearly represented by William Stern, who held that it is just merely a matter of measuring degrees of intelligence. Stern invented the I.Q. concept, which was a rating of degrees of intelligence or degrees of dominance, anxiety, and what not. That's been going on ever since. When I studied with Stern later in Hamburg, we developed the ascendence-submission dimension as an early personality test of the same sort. I liked to get at the dimensional aspects of values, and used the six values of Spranger as a base. I called these variables traits;

there was nothing original about that. The measure of various traits had been a project related to my doctoral research, so I was familiar with that from fairly early in the game. But to put a label of "trait psychology" on my work since then is to misrepresent it. I've been troubled by misinterpretation of the distinction between common traits and individual traits. At first I thought I could make clear the distinction between common traits, which are the abstracted trait categories we use for measuring personality, and the individual traits, which represent the way a given individual is actually organized. I found, however, that people merely doubled the use of the word "trait" and heard me to be suggesting traits again. Recently I've tried to change the terminology so that common traits would still be a valid field for research, but personal dispositions would focus on the morphogenic study of the individual in order to find out how he is organized.

EVANS: The way the word "trait" is sometimes used to describe generalized characteristics that might be more adequately described by the term "type" leads to the notion that there may be confusion about the differences in idiographic and nomothetic approaches[1] to the study of personality. How do you handle this problem?

ALLPORT: Recently I've been trying to propose the word "morphogenic" rather than idiographic, largely because people misspell idiographic. It's not derived

----

[1] In general, the terms have been applied to suggest that a nomothetic approach to psychology would seek general laws that apply to all individuals; idiographic, a focus on the individual as a unique entity.

from the base, "idea," but rather has the same root as idiosyncrasy, or "idio." I got tired of seeing misspellings, and thought that maybe morphogenic might express better the idea of things which originate in the person to explain his own form. We have morphogenic and molecular biology, and I think the parallel represents the distinction I'm trying to make in psychology. Molecular biology takes common elements and finds that almost all of life is made up of the same basic elements. That scientific framework is well advanced. The parallel dimension in psychology would be dimensional or differential or trait psychology. Morphogenic biology, however, is a little further behind as a science. We know very little about embryology, how organisms take a form and arrive at the peculiar structures they have. In psychology it's a particularly difficult problem as well because we're not trying to explain a species, but we're trying to explain the uniqueness of the person. That's what I call a morphogenic problem. It seems to me that to adequately distinguish these frames of reference, one could use nomothetic to mean general laws, principles, and dimensions, as opposed to morphogenic to mean the unique individual organism.

EVANS: You've made the point here that we should not become confused between common traits and the unique characteristics of the individual. You have, however, also written about central traits, cardinal traits, and secondary traits, and I wonder if you might distinguish among these for us.

ALLPORT: I didn't intend for these to become fixed

classificatory schemes at all. It is simply a means to
call attention to the fact that if you know one thing
about a person's trait system, you could predict his
attitude toward a great many other things. Gilbert
Chesterton said once about Tolstoy that if you knew
how he felt about the home rule bill, a pound of
tobacco, and a silk hat, you could predict his attitude
toward everything else because his whole philosophy
of life was directed toward what Chesterton called
"the simplification of life." We could call that a
cardinal trait in a man. Unique individuals have contributed very colorful words to our language, such
as Rabelaisian, Falstaffian, Quisling, or Xanthippe,
because they represent such outstanding characteristics devoted to a consistent mode of life. These
terms illustrate what I mean when I say we have
one focus, but most of us aren't so highly integrated.
Most people have some important foci of development, but we can usually distinguish six or eight,
and these would be more central traits. There would
likely be secondary ones which are not as well integrated as the others, as well as reflecting situational
and opportunistic expression. The trait categories I
postulated are meant to be a sort of continuum between the very central, central, and more peripheral
or accidental developments in the personality.

EVANS: As you describe your views of traits, Dr.
Allport, it begins to look as though you are really
more an antitrait theorist than a trait theorist in the
traditional sense, and I'm glad we have had an opportunity to make this distinction clear here. It would
be interesting also to see how you have used auto-

biographical material to analyze, by means of your approach to traits, the underlying personality of the individual.

ALLPORT: The biographer would have the same problem. He must use the English language, which is, of course, nomothetic in that every term has a general meaning, and yet with this language he must seek to establish the peculiar, unique organization of his subject. Ralph Barton Perry wrote a two-volume book on the thought and character of William James, and after two volumes of discussing the man and giving evidence in letters and quotations as to what he was like as a person, concluded the last chapter by saying that in order to understand James we really have to have four benign characteristics in mind and four somewhat semipathological characteristics in mind. Just to show what he means, you have to begin by understanding that James felt everything had truth in it, that his general conviction was that one could not be dogmatic and close the door to truth. I would call this a personal disposition. You wouldn't measure that or scale it in a general population because it is a personal outstanding central characteristic of James. But, on the other hand, he was rather hypochondriacal; that was one of the more pathological tendencies. It was interesting to me that Perry, after having a full knowledge of the man, said you have to understand eight dispositions to understand James, and then sums them up. This is just an example of how I think a biographer has to assume some theory of personality, and in this case, it happens to fit my own line of thinking. I do believe if you knew a few central things about the individual, you'd be able to predict most of his behavior. It's up to us to discover methods to find out what those personal dispositions are.

EVANS: Students in creative writing courses are often introduced to Freudian theory on the assumption that it might be a valuable tool with which to organize personality characterizations. It seems your system using traits would serve as another very excellent vehicle for a young writer to develop characters, plots, and so on. The distinctive feature of organizing character on the basis of your system would be that you emphasize the uniqueness of the individual rather than his conformity to a set pattern of characteristics. You emphasize the uniqueness of the individual also in your concept of motivation, and this is another concept in psychology which is of continuing interest. Many theorists still emphasize a biocentric theory of motivation which ascribes maintenance of the organism to physiological drives such as hunger, thirst, and so on, but allows for the development of various drives derived over time from these fundamental physiological drives. These would include the various social motives. It is about this point where your rather controversial concept of the functional autonomy of motives comes in. In your writings you have tried to explain that there are many drives, motives, or needs influencing our day-to-day behavior, which are not clearly derived from the primary drives; that they are for the individual functionally autonomous, and become self-sustaining. To illustrate this point, you had a generation of students rather seasick as they read your description of the sailor who went out to sea and remained there long after his early *original* needs for going out to sea were outgrown. His continuing urge to go out to sea you suggest is an illustration of functional autonomy. Would you care to elaborate on this notion?

ALLPORT: Let's begin with the problem engendered when I first used the term. I had no idea it would become controversial over the years. To me it was simply a way of stating what was perfectly obvious to me, that motives change and grow in the course of one's life. Our motivational structure is not today functionally dependent upon what we were at the age of three or four, or even fifteen. Motives change and grow, and I still can't understand why a person would challenge that basic proposition unless he were a die-hard believer in reactivity instead of proactivity, of homeostasis instead of transcendence, of balance or equilibrium instead of growth. But a person who is totally devoted to a stimulus-response view, I could understand, would not like the concept at all. To me it is more or less self-evident. I realized that it wasn't self-evident to others when I had to defend it and try to answer the very difficult question of how functional autonomy comes about. That leads us into the technical side of the picture. It seems to me to be an essential element to a sound theory of personality. Most theories stress the importance of events which occur early in life through conditioning, and the analytical theory requires that the life be traced backward in time. But people are busily living their lives forward; they are oriented

toward the future, and therefore, the psychologist
cannot be correct if he's oriented entirely to the past,
simply because his subject is not so oriented. One must
have some proactive view of human motivation to
explain plans and intentions, and self-image and long-
range goals, which are not like those of childhood,
and are not just conditioned reactions. They are pro-
actions and plans, and it seems to me to be basic to
a valid theory of personality that they be accounted
for.

EVANS: Just to illustrate how functional autonomy
works, could you give us an example of autonomous
motivation in operation?

ALLPORT: Let's take, for example, the phenomenon
of the son following in the father's profession, such
as politics. Several prominent families, such as the
Kennedys, LaFollettes, Tafts, and Roosevelts, have
had sons and grandsons follow in the family career
tradition. We would have to ask what are the current
motivations for the present generation. Supposing
they are fifty years old and have thrown themselves
into work in the Congress or legislature or what not—
what is their current motivation? I don't question
that they might have had a father identification when
they were six years old; most boys do. If daddy made
a speech, the son would play that he made a speech;
if daddy went to work, he would go out to work, too,
and so on. There is no doubt that such motivation
operates at an early age. But is that what sends
senators to the Senate to work hard for what they
believe in? Does their committee work represent an
attempt to be daddy at age fifty? It seems perfectly

ridiculous to me to believe that a normal person can be so motivated. But, giving Freud due credit, I can conceive of a neurotic who is still trying to step into daddy's shoes, or still trying to win mother's approval by making like daddy. But even if there is a possibility that a strictly neurotic individual might be so motivated, we would be able to distinguish this kind of neurotic motivation by its compulsive, inappropriate, and not age-related character.

It is necessary here to distinguish two types of functional autonomy which are necessary to get at the basic presuppositions of personality theory. This notion has been greatly criticized, and it has been welcome to me because it has forced me to rethink the matter somewhat. When people ask how functional autonomy comes about, I have to say there are two different levels. There is first a perseverated mechanism in the nervous system which is evident in repeated observations, that what has started tends to continue. The relay goes on; the cell assemblies fire and feed back and fire again. This kind of mechanism is well known even in lower animals, where you can establish a rhythm by training and then take away the training or the food or the reward, and the rhythm continues for a very long time.

EVANS: Like even after apparently extinguishing a response in an experimental animal, the response continues for a long time?

ALLPORT: Yes, and at the human level, we see that children are enormously repetitive. Until a child has something totally mastered, he wants it repeated over and over again exactly the same way. We see it with stories they wish read to them. Familiarity is something we all crave, and I think that it is a kind of feedback mechanism that, once established, continues to discharge itself. This kind of perseverated functional autonomy is a mechanism which feeds itself. But this does not fully satisfy me as a basis for behavior, even though it is true and can be demonstrated and should not be overlooked when developing a theory of personality. I think, however, that there is more to it than perseverated functional autonomy, and I labeled another kind of functional autonomy "propriate functional autonomy," which refers to oneself. Perseverated functional autonomy is still within the sphere of reactivity; something stimulates, feeds back, and stimulates again—the person is reacting to himself, his own circuits, and not to outside stimuli. But we are, after all, also proactive, and given to a kind of functional autonomy that responds to interests, goals, purposes, and relates warmly to one's sense of self. This is what I call propriate functional autonomy. If you ask me how it comes about, I would have to say merely that it is the nature of the human organism.

EVANS: As you suggest, some of those who have been critical of the notion of functional autonomy do, indeed, operate out of a more or less mechanistic theoretical orientation. So you have accounted for this mechanistic dimension of functional autonomy, but you still feel strongly that an adequate description of man requires that we have more than just the mechanistic view of him.

ALLPORT: Yes, that sums it very well. It's only

the people who are wedded to a totally reactive view of human behavior that would object violently to the idea of functional autonomy, and since I'm not wedded to that view, I can say that I see the need for both the reactive functional autonomy and the proactive functional autonomy as it operates in man.

EVANS: Your discussion of functional autonomy suggests that you would agree with the late Professor Kurt Lewin's (18) emphasis on a contemporaneous, ahistorical view of personality and motivation. Is this correct?

ALLPORT: Yes. I think Lewin and I both stress contemporaneity of motives. What drives the individual must drive him now, and if the past is at all relevant it has to be incorporated into the present. It must be active presently in the total field, if it's there at all. We do have memories and skills that we call on under specific motivational conditions, and so the past can be active in the present. I think that Lewin and I would agree that in normal behavior, the regions of the personality under tension at a given moment are the motives, and they are affected very much by the field or the situation that one is in. This presupposes a kind of fluid conception of the present motivational state of the person.

EVANS: Some of our colleagues in clinical psychology might find this notion of functional autonomy a little controversial, perhaps because of the concept of symptom removal as an end product of psychotherapy. You once used an example of an individual who had developed certain neurotic symptoms that might have been treated by a perfectly competent

psychoanalyst or psychotherapist. Through several
sessions, the patient might have been able to gain
deep-rooted insight into the cause of his neurotic
symptoms, but even though both patient and analyst
were apparently cooperating, the symptom persisted.
You might have interpreted this situation by saying
that perhaps the insight gained through therapy was
correct, but the behavior in question was functionally
autonomous; the patient had developed an intrinsic
need for the symptom per se, and no amount of
therapy would remove it because it was no longer
functionally related to its underlying cause.

ALLPORT: The relationship of functional autonomy
to neurosis is complicated. The best conclusion I've
been able to evolve is that if by retracing the life,
you cure the patient and eliminate the disorder, then
it certainly was not functionally autonomous. The
patient is simply acting out something that had been
repressed and was bothering him. A brief description
of a case involving a girl of twelve will illustrate
this point. She had a most annoying tic of smacking
her lips every few minutes or oftener, and though
it annoyed everyone, she could not stop it. She had a
kind of psychoanalysis which revealed that when she
was about three, her mother had told her that when
she breathed the air into her lungs, it was good air,
and when she breathed it out, it was bad air. This
worried her. It made her feel guilty because in breathing in good air and breathing out bad air, she must
be doing something to the air. She tried not breathing,
but that didn't work, and she didn't know what to
do about the guilt. So it occurred to her that when

a thing is hurt, you kiss it. Every time, therefore, she exhaled, she smacked her lips to kiss the air and make it well again. This process became pretty annoying after awhile, so pretty soon she seemed to have repressed the whole business. But she kept smacking her lips. Now, when this was worked through and explained to her, the tic vanished. I would say that the tic was being maintained there by an infantile complex of a sort, and the fact that it vanished indicates that it had not become part of the style of life of the person. However, in cases such as you mentioned, where no amount of analysis or retracing seems to eliminate the symptom, I would have to say that the symptom or the problem is the personality itself. It's the style of life which has been adopted for various reasons. It has gotten set; it means something; it fits the self-image somehow. Persons become ferociously possessive—mothers sometimes do—and they continue to be that way. No amount of insight would change it because jealousy has become a very important part of their style of life, and it is they; it's their personality.

EVANS: What you are saying here might be regarded as quite cynical by the advocates of the various kinds of psychotherapy. You are suggesting that some symptomatology becomes so entrenched that there is no way to break into the system and effect change.

ALLPORT: Well, I wouldn't agree with you that all psychotherapy is oriented toward a retracing to causation of symptoms. Psychoanalysis certainly does, and there may be others which operate out of this kind of backward theory. But there are also psychotherapeutic approaches which would attempt to break through the style of life that maintains an individual in an ineffective self-image. If you assume that the person is not happy with himself, you could, for example, examine the way that the person meets the world. You could use a Sullivanian approach that the trouble lies in disturbed interpersonal relationships, or you could approach it from a broader perspective and examine the self-concept of the person to find out why he has difficulty reconciling his needs and his ideals. Regardless of the approach one would take, I would say that all forms of psychotherapy are contemporaneous in that you attack the problem as it is at the moment and attempt to help the person to restructure the emphasis in his life and interests. There is just as much hope for a cure with this orientation as there is in the psychoanalytic approach of releasing blocked impulses through depth probing, perhaps even more.

EVANS: You mean, then, that if a symptom has become functionally autonomous for an individual, a historically oriented psychotherapy might not necessarily be effective in removing the symptom?

ALLPORT: Yes, I feel that some symptoms lend themselves better to one approach than another, so that a historically oriented therapy might aid one while others would be more susceptible to the situational technique.

EVANS: There are, however, some psychotherapists who would say that behaviors which seem to have outgrown the original drive or motive may still be

functions of experienced learning, and are not *really*
divorced from the original motive. They would account, therefore, for the apparently functionally autonomous symptom in terms of some form of higher-
order conditioning which has so reinforced the behavior in question that it persists.

ALLPORT: That's true, but this so-called secondary
reinforcement theory seems to me very shadowy and
not yet adequately proven or demonstrated. It is a
highly speculative sort of answer which requires that
the primary drive be reinforced somewhere along the
way. If you cannot demonstrate some reinforcing element, then you would have to say it's really functionally autonomous. A specific example will illustrate
what I mean. Say an infant's mother gives it comfort,
and it happens that her favorite color is blue, so that
the infant grows up predisposed to like blue. As
an adult he decorates his room in blue, wears blue
clothing, and so on. But now mother is dead and
gone, so what reinforcement can you maintain is
perpetuating his liking for blue? According to the
original theory, he would have to be comforted oc-
casionally in the presence of something blue, or his
mother, in order for the conditioning to become set.
In this case, we have gotten very removed from the
primary drive; so far removed, in fact, that it doesn't
make sense to say that the man now likes blue because
he was comforted at the age of two by a mother in
a blue dress. I would say he likes blue because he
likes blue. The historical story of this particular motivation to like blue could be as we have said, but

it doesn't explain what sustains the goal of surrounding himself with blue at age fifty, nor does it have to be reinforced by going back to the original pleasure that stamped it in.

EVANS: Functional autonomy was the subject of a series of "friendly arguments" between you and philosopher Peter Bertocci, of Boston University, which have become a classic dialogue in psychological and philosophical literature. How do you react to his criticisms of functional autonomy?

ALLPORT: Peter Bertocci is a good friend of mine and a professor of philosophy, but unlike some professors of philosophy, he reads psychology and tries to relate the philosophical presuppositions to the doctrine of the writer that he's studying. In the case of my work, he thinks that I can't defend the element of emergence that is inherent in the idea of functional autonomy. He sees that it requires a change, and not a retraining of the basic quality of the motive. He proposes that only an instinct doctrine of people born with directions which can be modified and overlaid and compounded can adequately explain personality. His objection, I believe, is largely that of a philosopher who wants continuity and can't accept the implication of discontinuity which my psychological framework may imply. However, I don't take his objections too seriously. He has also objected to my use of ego as an evolving portion of personality rather than as a given element, and this is a similar kind of objection. He thinks that unless we're born with a self, we can't create one. The child must have the capacity for selfhood from the beginning, as he sees it; but these are more philosophical difficulties, and I manage to hold my ground fairly well on the matter.

EVANS: The same growth factor that you postulate as necessary for functional autonomy would be needed to describe the concepts of self and ego, and in fact, focusing on ego autonomy is one important contemporary approach to understanding personality. Your concept of propriate, which relates to self and ego, while it imples this growth factor, doesn't appear to be exactly the same as ego or exactly the same as self. It seems to have a unique quality. I wonder if you would elaborate on this.

ALLPORT: Before I try to explain what I mean by propriate, I probably should tell why I took that term instead of ego or self, which are more familiar. Back in the 1880s, psychology texts were organized with chapters dealing with segmental aspects of personality, and then a final chapter dealing with the self or soul, which was to account for the unity or coherence in a life. Usually it turned out to be a question-begging explanation where anything you couldn't account for any other way was attributed to the self or the soul. It was not a very clearheaded approach. In 1890, William James (16) wrote his famous chapter on the self, which was so good and so definitive that I think nobody tried for several decades to improve on it, and were careful to avoid the question-begging element in their later expositions of self-concept. The notion practically disappeared from psychology until about the 1940s to 1950s, except in very special uses like the way some schools of psychology used it. Freud, of course, had used the term ego, but in a very limited sense as the knower that tried to make the homeostatic adjustment to the id and the superego and to the external environment. So, we see that with few exceptions, the word ego itself did not exist in systematic psychology. In the early 1940s, I found myself preparing a review of experimental literature where something like the self or self-involvement or ego-involvement was a parameter in the experiment. Students were asked, for example, to answer a lot of questions by telling them that we were developing a new test and would like to get their reactions. Under this condition, they were not particularly ego-involved. If, however, we instructed them that the test was important to their record and would be sent to the dean's office, and so on, they became ego-involved, and not merely task-involved. Experiments of this sort, where there were two variables, turned out to have very large percentage differences in the results when the person was ego-involved or merely operating on a peripheral or opportunistic level. I wrote a paper (4) about this type of experiment which helped, I think, to reestablish the respectability of a concept such as self or ego-involvement.

EVANS: Your investigation into this aspect of personality may have brought the notion of self or self-awareness as a construct back into the ranks of the "respectable fold" of academic psychology, while allowing for some of the theorists who were exponents of this concept to come back into the forefront as well.

ALLPORT: I hadn't thought of it that way, but that may be true. I did, I think, establish the fact that you've got a perfectly objective operational parameter which gives you differential results in behavior, and therefore is a valid approach to the study of personality. Since that time, there have been about three fairly recent presidential addresses at the National Psychological Association that quite unashamedly reintroduced the self in various contexts. But to explain why I tried not necessarily to avoid the term, but why I have coined the term "proprium," and especially the adjectival form, "propriate," I would say that in the literature I found at least eight different uses or definitions of ego and self. Both terms are practically interchangeable by different authors, so I don't think we can make a systematic distinction, even though all the meanings were acceptable. To avoid the question-begging approach involved in the usage of the words self or ego, I felt that we might take a word that is fresh so that every time it was used it wouldn't have to be defined, nor would it be cluttered with the baggage of former connotations of self or ego. But in my books, I do use self, especially in relation to the development of the self or sense of self evolving from childhood, and I feel it is an important construct.

EVANS: George Herbert Mead's distinction between the self as an actor and the self as an object is an example of this developmental model as well, is it not?

ALLPORT: These are two of eight that I found.

EVANS: The developmental approach to the concept

of self is not as broad in perspective as the notion of proprium as you have proposed it. What often happens when some one proposes a term that has growth connotations in psychology is that some individuals accuse him of being transcendental or even metaphysical, and while I'm certain you had no intention of proposing a metaphysical concept, I wonder how you would defend the concept of proprium against this kind of criticism.

ALLPORT: Anyone who says it's transcendental or mystical just hasn't read what I've written. I stated very carefully that the idea of an agent, a separate agent, whether metaphysical or mystical, is not what I intended. I've often said that proprium is an entirely operational construct which is necessary and can't be avoided in a systematic personality theory. I would define proprium in terms which might be considered phenomenological by saying it's that part of the personality which seems to be warm and central to the person, involving matters that are of importance in this life over and above the mere matters of fact in it. If you begin from the phenomenological core it can be demonstrated that this sense of proprium, when it is present, makes an operationally demonstrable difference in behavior. Thus, I don't consider it to be a mystical conception at all.

EVANS: There are whole categories of psychological concepts that lend themselves to the charge of being metaphysical, and in fact, a theorist who is not pretty mechanistic in his orientation is often accused personally of not being a "scientist." American psychology has been greatly influenced by the need to be operational and scientific. Would you agree that there is such a thing as being operational or scientific to a fault in our field?

ALLPORT: Oh, I think there is. I used the term operational simply to point out the fact that there is a demonstrable difference in behavior which is ego-involved and that which is not ego-involved. You can point to the experiment that proves it and give the quantity of difference in the conduct. So, in a sense, you can establish the proprium operationally. On the other hand, I am no admirer or worshipper of the concept of operationalism, because whenever we're trying to become operational from facts of experience which can't be made objective enough to satisfy a strict positivist or operationalist, they say it's meaningless. I don't think it's meaningless at all—nothing in human experience is meaningless. But I don't think we give up studying a thing just because you can't satisfy the most rigid tests of operationalism.

EVANS: As soon as we discuss terms such as proprium, self, or ego we begin to relate to the existentialist or phenomenological points of view introduced into psychology by individuals such as Robert McCleod and Rollo May, who reflect the influence of the entire existentialist or phenomenological movement involving thinkers such as Tillich, Sartre, Heidegger, or Husserl. The notions of phenomenology or existentialism cause us to ask to what degree must a psychologist be concerned with "under the skin" facets of the individual. Might we, for instance, go too far in introducing such nonoperational frames of reference into the science of psychology?

ALLPORT: To say that we go too far is a matter of subjective judgment. I think we can go a good deal farther than we have before we've exhausted the value that comes from reports of experience when it's done thoroughly. We've neglected subjective reports in psychology so long that I'm not immediately worried about being too phenomenological.

CURRENT AREAS OF INTEREST IN PSYCHOLOGY

Neurophysiology

Genetic Determinants of Personality Versus Social-Environmental Determinants

Existentialism

The Nature of Prejudice

Personality and Religion

Maturity, Aging, and Mental Health

Personality Testing

The Study of Values

Philosophy of Training Psychology Students

"Scientism" and Significant Research

Action Research

Objectivity in the Study of Personality

Open Versus Closed Systems

Use of Autobiographies

PART III

Overview | In this section I confront Dr. Allport with a number of questions relating to areas of contemporary interest to psychologists. He presents his reaction to the importance of neurophysiology, the controversial genetic versus social and environmental influences on personality, and existentialism. He also discusses his famous work dealing with the nature of prejudice. As one psychologist who was always willing to come to grips with the role of religion in personality development, his reactions to questions in this area are quite provocative. He also discusses his views of maturing, aging, and mental health. His response to questions concerning personality testing provide a good opportunity to examine his resolution of the problem of personality testing. We discuss his widely used test which measures interests and values, the Allport-Lindzey-Vernon Study of Values, and talk about whether a preoccupation with the scientific method in psychology can really lead to significant research. As perhaps one of the most influential teachers in the history of psychology, Dr. Allport's reactions to my questions concerning the proper focus in the training of psychology students are particularly interesting. He also answers questions dealing with other areas of interest such as action research, objectivity in the study of personality, closed versus open systems of psychological theory, and the use of autobiographical materials which he illustrated in such a fascinating way in his study of *Letters from Jenny*.

EVANS: Dr. Allport, other advances in psychology stem from the work in neurophysiology. Many attempts are being made to correlate specific brain centers with behavioral responses, and since you refer to neuropsychic mechanisms as some sort of brain or central nervous system factor in personality, I wonder if you feel that this neurophysiological psychology might be a fruitful field for research?

ALLPORT: Yes, indeed. I am not a physiological psychologist myself, but I would hope that we might ultimately converge our best theoretical empirical thinking with tests and behavioral evidence demonstrated by the neurophysiologist. I'm always interested in reading what Hebb, Penfield, Olds, and so on are contributing. It may be selective perception on my part, but it seems to me that what they are finding enforces the importance of a kind of high-level gaiting, which would fit perfectly into my conception of personal dispositions.

EVANS: An interesting prob-

lem which permeates some of our theoretical thinking in psychology deals with this notion of levels
of analysis. Some such work as that of your colleague,
Dr. Skinner, emphasizes only operant conditioning;
other work such as that of Hebb is concerned with
physiological mechanisms; while individuals such as
Abraham Maslow or Carl Rogers want to focus primarily on human experience. These differing levels of
analysis once again tend to force the psychologist to
come to grips with the mind-body problem. In fact, it's
not too popular anymore even to talk about it. I believe we already touched on this briefly earlier in our
discussion.

ALLPORT: I doubt that I could solve the mind-body
problem in the next few minutes, but it is a problem
which students of psychology should be aware of,
along with other problems relevant to the presuppositions that psychologists make. My own point of
view is that the neurological level and the personality
level and the conscious experiential level do relate
to one another, and perhaps there is a kind of isomor-
phic relationship in that what goes on at one level
also goes on at others. But these activities will all
involve different feelings; you can't see consciousness;
you can't see into the brain to know what's going
on there; so they involve very complex relationships.
And there's little known about them. Dr. Stern used to
say that they could be related by way of the person,
and that the fundamental entity, the fundamental
unit, is the person. He, of course, tried to account for
both body and mind, neurological and psychic, and
attempted to find a tertium quid, a third factor which

would be the relational link between body and mind. But I'm not sure that that's the solution. The two are, I believe, closely related, and in time it may be possible to make that relationship clear.

EVANS: Another historical stalemate which has not yet been solved is the nature-nurture question, though breaking of the genetic code may eventually shed vast new lights on this issue. In fact, the effects of DNA and RNA have already been demonstrated to have far-reaching significance for psychology as well as the biological sciences.

ALLPORT: You've indicated another absolutely baffling, but basic, issue here. There's no doubt that genetic dispositions are primary determinants, and we know practically nothing about them. It's for this reason, I believe, that American psychology has been so heavily environmentalistic. Watson's saying, "Give me a baby and I'll make practically anything out of it, butcher, baker, or candlestick maker," is a reflection of the heavily environmentalistic framework of American psychology. I just don't know what the future holds, but in this area, our knowledge is a drop, and our ignorance is a sea. I believe, however, that we'll never have a complete psychology of personality until we have a much better knowledge of genetic factors.

EVANS: Do you feel that the discoveries being made in molecular biology, for example, will shed new insight into the nature of the individual?

ALLPORT: It's the first step in that direction, although there has been very little relevant research in this direction. The most significant research for psychology is the identical twin work which has dealt mostly with the development of traits and personal dispositions that may have genetic determination. There has been some evidence that identical twins develop similar personalities, especially in the region of introverted and extraverted dispositions. We've got to know that sort of thing before we can know just what causes the personality to develop as it does. Environment is very important, but I am simply saying that we've neglected the genetic factor because we don't know much about it.

EVANS: Psychologists sometimes accuse sociologists of going too far afield in emphasizing the social environment of the developing individual (as we discussed briefly earlier), yet the socialization process is obviously an important aspect of the so-called heredity-environment question, and while there may be a lot of pseudotheory operating in the laymen's view of this issue, the question is significant for the psychology of personality. Would you care to comment here about the socialization process as you see it as a parameter in personality?

ALLPORT: This, again, is a very basic question, and one which reveals how little we know about the subtleties of the process by which the child acquires cultural or family tradition. We're almost totally ignorant of the way the child internalizes or rejects cultural traditions and develops his own version of the forces acting upon him. Even though we know that the parents are the most important single factor in the child's life, we don't know much about how their influence is felt, whether through subtle cues, or meanings, or what not. I don't think traditional learning theory is adequate to explain this either, because the child doesn't always perform according to theory; that is, he doesn't always do what he's rewarded for, nor avoid what he's punished for. The attitude life of the child is much more subtle, and I think acquired through cues and meanings from subtle behavior of the parents, but we don't know much about it. Freud put the emphasis on emotional identification with the parent. That was his only theory of learning, and I think this is a factor, but by no means the only factor. We have much to learn yet about the socialization process.

EVANS: We can't help but raise the question of the importance of the concept of parental rejection in the socialization process. Studies of delinquents and schizophrenics alike indicate that there is a history of parental rejection in their past. On the other hand, research investigating the development of creativity indicates that some highly creative persons also have been rejected by their parents. This conflict causes one to wonder how useful the idea of parental rejection really is in assisting us in understanding the socialization process.

ALLPORT: The best that I can do, I suppose, is to say that X percentage of those who had a certain kind of upbringing turn out to be delinquent and a wide percentage of those of another type do so, and so on. It's just a probabilistic statement, and doesn't explain what goes on in the individual child. Two brothers will develop very differently, though they are both exposed to the same type of parental influence. Even though we know all the factors that are affecting a child, the most important single thing, individual reactions, we cannot predict.

EVANS: When we examine a developmental model such as Freud's which postulated that the child at first is irrationally nondiscriminating and emerges slowly to a point where its own rationality begins to govern its behavior, we encounter the same problem of determinism. Even though the child has evolved what Adler called a style of life, he still seems to have introjected a great deal from his period of development when he was essentially dominated by irrational behavior. Can we accept such notions of the effects of early influences on present behavior? Certainly, virtually all contemporary developmental models, with the possible exception of Piaget's (which views the child as being in a sense rational from the beginning), stress the importance of these chaotic early influences.

ALLPORT: We must look for truth somewhere in the middle. We sometimes, I think, much overdo the emphasis on early life. A factor important to the socialization process which has not yet been mentioned is the self-image of the individual. Lecky tells of a case that illustrates the point. Here's a child that has grown up to the age of six and is still a thumb-sucker. Nothing has stopped it—bitter aloes, punishment, reward, bandages, nothing. He's just a chronic thumb-sucker. But suddenly, he stops sucking his thumb, and when he was asked why, he said, "Big boys don't suck their thumb." In other words, it suddenly came through to him that he was a big boy and that didn't fit with his present thumb-sucking style of life. This may happen at six, at ten, or even at twenty or sixty. One's conception of what one is, one's proper style of life, must fit into the present style of being, and is an important factor in making or breaking habits and in forming attitudes, and so on. This is a factor in learning which is very much neglected, and I don't think this self-image factor ceases to develop after childhood.

EVANS: You're really emphasizing the importance of the proprium and the integral concepts of self-growth and self-development, and that the process of socialization cannot be considered to be an irrational process imposed on a passive receiver. There must be some integrative mechanism, and the developing child must be active in the process.

ALLPORT: Individuals are in a constant process of becoming. Many factors enter into the process, including some mechanical learning out of habits from the past, but all these factors must be accounted for when we attempt to determine how personality becomes what it is. We may learn to keep to the right in traffic or how to run a machine or some skill which might be explained by traditional theory, but the concept of becoming includes also the self-image, maturation, identification, and all forms of cognitive learning. They must all be accounted for in an adequate theory of personality.

EVANS: You made the point in your book, *Becoming* (7), that personality grows in a continuing way and we cannot break up development into segments such as the first five years, the next five years, and so on. Emergent personality must be taken as a total process of development.

ALLPORT: Goldstein (15) and Maslow (20) have been trying to say the same thing using the concept of self-actualization. They feel that as long as a person lives, he has to actualize his being, and it doesn't stop at any period, nor is it fixed or set at any given episode of life.

EVANS: You would be inclined to agree, then, with Jung's discussion of the individuation process. He felt that individuation is an important process even into middle age, and his ideas are consistent with the emergence of the existential movement in that the individual begins to raise questions of "who am I," "what am I here for," and so on. Do you feel that it is a healthy thing for the individual to become more and more preoccupied with thoughts of his own existence?

ALLPORT: When you raise questions about aging, you almost invite me to speak introspectively, but I realize that you are getting at the increased length of life which allows a man more time for such questions. The retirement age of sixty-five was set by Bismarck nearly a hundred years ago, but is no longer applicable because the average life expectancy is thirty years more now than in his time. However that may be, there has been an increase in interest in the psychological process of aging. I would say that there are probably as many ways of aging as there are individuals because I argue for uniqueness at every stage of being. The Hindu psychologists tell us that it is very characteristic of older people to seek a fourth stage of life which is called meaning or liberation, but represents a disengagement from the activities of the first stages that are more pleasure- and success-seeking and doing one's duty. The fourth stage is the one you referred to which brings up the questions, "who am I," "what's it all about," "what next," and so on. It's a natural concern as one grows older, but not peculiar to old age alone. Perhaps it's characteristic of our times that the question will have a more subjective, personal tone to it. The Aristotelians asked the question, "what is man" and that led to all the sciences of man, but we today are asking it more personally, as "who am I." This shift of emphasis is part of the so-called existential trend of our times, and I don't think it's either good or bad, though it's probably good because we have a right to know the answer to both the questions, "what is man" and "who am I." It's not a question strictly of concern to the older person either because youth is interested in it as well.

EVANS: To ask such questions as these tends to put pressure on the individual to find answers to them. This causes one to speculate on the differences between the individual who asks such questions of himself and the one who never in his lifetime finds occasion to raise them. Some people never arrive at a stage where they are even concerned with the problem of being, and it causes one to wonder if the mere asking of such a question implies a degree of maturity that others have not attained.

ALLPORT: My one criticism of the existential movement is that it tends to be rather egghead and philosophical and ascribes to all human beings the same existential vacuum. The eggheads and the elite would give to all men their own anxiety, nausea, and alienation. It reminds me of the co-ed who says, "I can't tell you how much I enjoyed my existential anxiety." I just don't think it's true that every man goes through this anxiety and anguish and alienation in his effort to find meaning. Empirically and factually, you find a lot of personalities who live their lives without worrying about it. However, as the educational level increases, more people read more books, and ponder more the questions they encounter, and I suppose it's natural to have more and more of this type of concern.

EVANS: It's interesting that you suggest that this whole existential question could be the product of an intellectual culture. It implies that we may have a sampling problem here which reflects both an intellectual and a cultural orientation. Though the question of existence is dealt with differently by different religions, another problem with existentialism is that it is very loosely defined. Each writer defines it differently and it may be that its only definition comes from within the individual and can't really be intellectualized at all.

ALLPORT: The movement is a broad one, of course, and solutions have been offered from both the atheistic and from the theistic points of view. Some stress alienation and some stress the need for commitment and responsibility; some search for meaning, and others for different things. There are many shades and flavors of it, but it's a movement highly characteristic of our times. It's rather lately come to

America, but the American version has a little less of the pessimistic or fatalistic flavor than the European existentialism. America has produced her own existentialists, but they are generally more hopeful that in confronting the mysteries of life, even when starting with anguish and despair, one can work out a commitment and a solution adequate to himself. Rogers' approach is a kind of home-grown existentialism and typically American in its optimism; its flavor is rather different from the pessimistic. There are varieties of approaches to this question which seem to be concerning more and more of the population, but I feel, because of the student involvement in it, that it did originate with the elite.

EVANS: Wherenever a movement of this type emerges, there are those who will say that this, too, is a passing phenomenon, and that generations hence will be concerned with some other theological or philosophical problems. Do you feel that man will arrive at a stage in development where he will become increasingly less concerned with this existential question?

ALLPORT: The history of ideas has always been a reflection of historical conditions: plagues, wars, etc. The danger of the atomic bomb and the terrible tragedies which it implies has thrown this century into a kind of reflective mood. I have no doubt that there is a historical determination. But Tillich points out in his book, *The Courage To Be* (25), that there has been a rise and fall over the centuries. One age was preoccupied with guilt, where earlier ages dealt with ontological guilt, and there might now be more preoccupation with meaning, and the question, "what does it all mean." There are different kinds of pre-occupations that concern each age. Death, Tillich (25) says, was a concern of the Greeks, and it's still a concern of ours, though we are more interested in the meaning of suffering than in just the tragedy of death. I am inclined to think it's a sign of growing maturity to ask the question "who am I"; to ask whence and whither, without being overcome by the need to adjust to the realities of technological advances. It puts more strain on the personality to do the adapting and the socializing and to continue to meet the economic problems of life while at the same time going on as a human being to think about one's own nature and destiny.

EVANS: Now to move to another major area of discussion, Dr. Allport. You've contributed a great deal over the years to the understanding of prejudice. Perhaps we might begin by asking you to define prejudice.

ALLPORT: Oddly enough, the best definition for prejudice is a slang one: "Prejudice is being down on something you're not up on." It has two features, both of which are essential ingredients: being down on something means that you are hostile and negative or rejecting of the object in question; and there is the logical error or cognitive mistake because it is always false. We can be down on something that we are up on, too. We can be against criminals, assassins, Hitler's gang, and so forth; and for good reasons—because they violate our values—we are up on them.

But in prejudice there is always an element of igno-rance—unwarranted hostility—or else it's not preju-dice. To put it in more dignified terms, let's use Thomas Aquinas' definition that prejudice is "thinking ill of others without sufficient warrant," which means exactly the same thing. Prejudice must be defined as having two variables—one is hostility, and one is ignorance or erroneous judgment. Otherwise you don't have prejudice. Let me add, of course, that there can be prejudice in favor of others. Spinoza spoke of love prejudice and hate prejudice. I've only defined hate prejudice here, but the psychologists' love prejudices would be the same thing—thinking well of others without sufficient warrant.

When I wrote *The Nature of Prejudice* (6), the problem of causation was so large that it took several years for me to figure out the table of contents for the book. However, the table of contents that emerged satisfies the question of causes, but even so, there are a large number of chapters because there are a great many causes. There is no single, simple thing that causes people to be prejudiced. I've divided the causes into rough levels for the purpose of analysis: historical, sociocultural, character and personality fac-tors, perceptual factors, and the qualities of the victim himself. For example, if you don't know anything about the history of slavery in this country, you wouldn't know much about the nature of current preju-dice. And on the sociocultural level, factors including a way of life that gets established must be included with some of the distal factors which are actually translated into behavior. Psychologically, elements which entered into the character, structure of personality, attitude, and training of the individual must be considered, while perceptual elements such as the way individualism in the minority group is perceived are important. Finally, you must take into account the qualities of the victim himself because sometimes his behavior is perceived more or less corruptly and it puts an element of factuality into the judgment which may or may not support his prejudice. It's a very complicated question which would have to include perhaps eighteen to twenty distinguishable causal factors.

EVANS: And you see that these factors originate both from within the individual, his psychological makeup, and from the environment or culture in which the individual operates, resulting in a wide variety of interactive effects.

ALLPORT: Yes, but I would emphasize that the historical and sociocultural factors have to be translated into the nervous system of the individual. They don't act automatically. The term that is missing here to describe the interaction is conformity. We have never answered why people pick up the historical and sociocultural traditions and translate them into attitudes and behavior. I realize that what I propose is a psychologically biased point of view because I am a psychologist. I often argue with my colleagues in sociology and anthropology because they don't think that the psychological is important; they feel the problem can be handled by studying the traditions and demographic variables which impinge on it. I feel, however, that even all those variables must be filtered through human beings and in being filtered through, they become habits and attitudes. This is just my psychological bias.

EVANS: Another question integrally related to prejudice is the concept of discrimination, toward the elimination of which we are spending a great deal of energy in our country. As late as 1954 in *Brown* versus *The Board of Education,* it was probably the first time in history that a social or behavioral science perspective was influential in a significant Supreme Court decision. Yet government can only attempt to eliminate discrimination through legal manipulation of the cultural supports for it. Would you, with your orientation toward the individual, be satisfied that merely changing the environment through legal means would be an effective means to cut down prejudice and/or discrimination?

ALLPORT: I would concede here a little to my sociological colleagues. If it's a matter of attitudes and prejudices, will we not have to effect changes in the education and exhortation of children to make long-range changes in prejudice? It does not seem to follow from what I have previously said because when an external situation is changed by fiat or through law, you may have eliminated discrimination but you have not necessarily also eliminated prejudice. These two are not the same thing. After discrimination has been eliminated and people come into equal-status contact with one another, then their attitudes may be affected away from prejudice. I would not, of course, rule out intercultural education, or exhortation, or working with individuals, but I really feel it's more efficient to begin with a large-scale change in the social structure. At least this approach will eliminate discrimination and eventually, I believe, alleviate prejudice.

EVANS: Do you use the terms discrimination and prejudice in the same way that Gerhard Saenger (23), the social psychologist, did? He distinguished them by saying that discrimination is really a behavioral manifestation, an act, while prejudice seems to be more internal or cognitive.

ALLPORT: Yes, as I see it, discrimination simply denies people rights and privileges that they want which represents a social, external act, but a feeling state such as prejudice is not relevant to that because a lot of people who have very little prejudice will discriminate when they're in a situation that calls for discrimination.

EVANS: Would you say that the same differentiating categories could be applied to the terms integration and desegregation, in that integration would be more of a psychological process, while desegregation would be more social?

ALLPORT: It would seem that these are both sociological terms. Integration is not used in a psychological sense, and therefore cannot be too readily applied as a psychological concept. As I understand it, desegregation means you make a token concession and integration means you really buckle down and do the job. It wouldn't seem to be quite the same distinction applied to prejudice and discrimination.

EVANS: Somewhat related to our discussion of prejudice is the notion of an individual's system of beliefs, or ideology, on which there has been con-

siderable research emphasis during the last twenty
years. While this research presents a more molar problem than does research dealing with such areas as
racial or religious prejudice, some interesting work
has been done in an effort to expand our understanding of ideologies. One of the early major works of this
type was, of course, *The Authoritarian Personality*
(1). It has been criticized because it was felt that
the investigators reflected too much of their own
values in it, and somewhat divided the world into
"good guys" and "bad guys"; everything found in the
study on which the book is based relating to au-
thoritarians appears to be undesirable; everything relating to equalitarians appears to be desirable.

ALLPORT: I believe the publication of *The Authoritarian Personality* in 1950 stirred up the social
sciences, particularly social psychology, perhaps more
than any book published in this century. There have
been many attacks upon it, many attempts to replicate
it, and many uses of the E-scale for ethnocentrism
and the F-scale for authoritarianism. The last I
counted, there were some 500 studies based on this
work, and there have been more since then. I am
sure that there is residual truth here, in that authoritarian ideology presents the same problems to
the investigator as does religion. But it is worth
working on. I have regretted that I haven't been
able to work in this area, but there are so many
aspects of personality that one person can't work
on all of them. I have been an admirer of that book,
even though there are shortcomings in it. It's true that
the book was written by liberals, and the very fact

that they called the authoritarian personality "F,"
measured by the F-scale which stood for Fascist, reflects the historical times. You remember that this
work was going on before the end of World War II
when everyone was anti-Hitler and everything he
stood for, and it was to some extent a cultural product.
In time, the distortions resulting from artifacts or
errors of measurement will be ironed out and the
residual truth will remain. It represents a work which
will have a basic residual contribution to social
psychology.

EVANS: Along this line is the work done by Milton
Rokeach (21), who suggests that dogmatism is really
the underlying factor; that authoritarianism is the
same whether it is on the left or on the right. He
felt that the pattern was the same, whether the person
was dogmatic Freudian or dogmatic liberal. It represents a change in the notion that open-mindedness
is necessarily connected with the "left" and closed-
mindedness is necessarily connected with the "right."

ALLPORT: This seems to have been one of the
errors of *The Authoritarian Personality*, and I believe
that Rokeach was right about the matter. One could
be dogmatic or authoritarian or closed-minded on
almost any issue and it would seem that the psy-
chodynamics are probably very similar.

EVANS: Dr. Rokeach wasn't attempting to place a
good or bad connotation on the terms open- or closed-
mindedness, but was attempting to show that the
pattern might be present with or without respect to
the values involved. But there may yet be a hidden
value system operating within psychology which puts

a premium on open-mindedness and criticizes closed-mindedness. In fact, Dr. James Hillman, of the Analytic Institute in Zurich, once asked me why it is that Americans put such a premium on being open-minded about things. He questioned whether it were possible for Americans to be certain or dogmatic or sure about anything. It raises the question of whether tolerance in and of itself is necessarily a virtue.

ALLPORT: Bertrand Russell says, "an open mind is bound to be an empty mind." But this is a good question. I think we have semantic problems with words like open and closed, and Fascist and liberal, and so on, and we've got to come to some understanding here. In the December 1963 issue of the *Journal of Abnormal and Social Psychology*, there is an article by Kellman and an associate that interprets authoritarianism as the degree to which an individual has breadth of perspective. The truly authoritarian person cannot live without a security system and safety islands and a narrow orbit of thought; he lacks breadth of perspective; he can't be tentative. Kellman puts it more in a cognitive perspective of closeness in the sense that the authoritarian cannot live with hypothetical and ambiguous situations. The opposite to that would resemble what the California group[1] would call the democratic or antiauthoritarian, and is a person who can live with ambiguities and un-

---

[1] The "California Group" refers to sociologist T. W. Adams and psychologists Else Frenkel-Brunswik, Nevitt Sanford, and Daniel Levinson, who jointly authored and completed research for *The Authoritarian Personality.*

certainties. He can realize that the other guy might be right or at least that the other guy has a right to life and liberty, and his perspective is a little more broad and flexible. I don't think a man's degree of authoritarianism is functionally related to his degree of commitment. Every one must have a commitment or a set of values to live by, but it is conceivable that a person could be so open-minded that he doesn't have any commitment. In that case he would be hopeless.

EVANS: You're suggesting, however, that one could have a very firm commitment and still, within the framework of that commitment, be liberal, tolerant, open-minded, or whatever term you choose, and that commitment and open-mindedness may not be incompatible at all.

ALLPORT: Yes. I had a Ph.D. thesis submitted to me last year that dealt with the relationship between self-objectification and commitment. Ernest Keen, who made the study, wondered to what degree a person could see himself with scientific detachment as a specimen who has been to some extent determined by his environment and education. The question was whether a man could look at himself objectively as a specimen and at the same time firmly believe in certain values. He found people in all of the four cells; there were those who could objectify themselves but didn't have much in the way of commitment and therefore they were pretty cynical and opportunistic about life. Similarly, you find people with commitments but no self-objectification. They tend to be fanatic and would probably fall into the authoritarian category because they can't stand off at all and see themselves in perspective.

EVANS: Is this somewhat similar to Henry Murray's concept of anti-intraceptiveness, which he defined as the defensive inability to gain insight into one's self and others?

ALLPORT: They are related, and I feel that Murray meant the kind of an interest in human nature and human qualities and foibles which would be associated with self-objectification, since a person interested in other people's thought would logically also be interested in his own.

EVANS: Closely related to the notion of commitment is the whole question of religion and the part it plays in the personality structure. There are some who feel that psychologists are not sympathetic to religion, but you have given the subject a great deal of thought and exposition. How do you feel that religion fits into the study of personality?

ALLPORT: The study of religious values is an outgrowth of my interest in personality theory, which is the basic concern out of which all my professional work has come. In 1937, I postulated a general theoretical approach in my book, *Personality: A Psychological Interpretation* (2), but since then a lot of special problems have arisen that must be dealt with: what is the nature of attitudes in personality structure; what can you do with personal documents; what is the formation of prejudice that makes it so central to personality structure; what about some of the major values, etc. The work I did on the Study of Values

Test is an aspect of the interest in more complex levels of personality. Religion, obviously, belongs in that same category as one of the complex sentiments that many, if not most, people develop. It represents a problem of personality—perhaps a specialized part of personality—and I think it's ridiculous for a psychologist to neglect it or overlook its importance in the structure of personality. Some years ago I was looking over a widely used textbook in psychology, and I found only one reference to religion in the entire book. Mind you, this was a book on man's nature, and in it there was but one reference to religion. I looked up that reference and found that it said the phrenologists used to think that the faculty of religion was located in the brain, but that the area was presently believed to be devoted to the operation of the knee jerk. That was the only mention of religion in the book. I submit that this is a thoroughly ridiculous and inadequate treatment of such an important sentiment in personality. In order to bring religion into line with a comprehensive study of personality, I presented six lectures on the subject which were later published in the book, *The Individual and His Religion* (5). This may have been the study you referred to.

EVANS: Would you summarize some of the main ideas you presented in those lectures to give us an insight into how you feel about the religious dimension of personality?

ALLPORT: I think it is helpful to take the developmental approach in this study. A child is totally incapable of understanding the abstraction of theology, and so he takes on the family religion simply as a matter of course, just as he takes to brushing his teeth or speaking the English language or taking on political sentiments. This is particularly true during the period of his close family identification between ages eight and eleven or so. He just follows the family pattern. Ordinarily the normal child begins after a while to question the family pattern simply because the statements are obviously abstract, and some of them sound rather outrageous to his literal-minded ears. Usually he goes through a period of questioning, but it's not that he's questioning religion as such. He's questioning what he thought his parents taught; he's questioning the dogmas as he understood them, not as the parents understood them. He's questioning his own childish approach, and that is the essential element for any personality if it is eventually to grow up. There are some, of course, in whom the childish formations and beliefs don't change; they go through life with essentially a juvenile, undeveloped religion. But about sixty percent, I should say, of the college students report having a very acute adolescent rebellion. What happens to them after that is subject to a wide variety of differential influences, and the personality develops in an individual style.

EVANS: The adolescent rebellion you refer to here is rebellion against what they believe to be some of the basic dogmas of religion?

ALLPORT: Yes, I'm glad you made that point clear. What I mean is that their childish understanding is no longer tenable because it was acquired in tiny bits and fragments and was interpreted in childish ways. The adolescent thinks it's the parent's fault, so it takes its place among other emotional upheavals or rebellions he undergoes in his attempt to get away from parental domination. When I speak of adolescent rebellion, therefore, I really am referring to the reaction against the childish beliefs that gets mixed up with the rather ordinary general rebellion against parental domination. In this situation, the religion that the adolescent has learned goes under. Very often there are acute religious feelings because of the new experiences that the adolescent goes through in trying to find his identity and his place in the world and the meaning of the mysteries of things. He's often religious, but in a turmoil. Then later he attempts to resolve this turmoil by a variety of means, such as adopting the same attitude his parents had when he has children of his own. He begins to think that on the whole the parents didn't do so badly after all, and this tends to resolve the conflict for him. This phenomenon often occurs around the age of thirty or so. The twenties are perhaps the least religious age of man.

EVANS: Several early studies investigating the effects of religion in the individual personality found a high correlation between religiosity and prejudice, which would seem to indicate that religion was narrowing the individual. Still our later study (11) has suggested that there might be two aspects of religion which operate differentially on the individual; the one reflected in more humanitarian concerns while the other is reflected in a more selfish aspect of religion. Do you feel that this notion, opening the possiblity of a differential impact of religion, is consistent with your experience?

ALLPORT: We are presently engaged in a research project which deals with this very question. It's a design to study the relation between religion and prejudice. It's not surprising that the early studies revealed the results they did because the concepts of religion were somewhat ambiguous in the early tests. All research indicates that churchgoers on the average are much more prejudiced than nonchurchgoers, and that's a fact. It would seem to be a curious finding in view of the fact that most of the people who have devoted themselves to brotherhood are religiously motivated, and some good examples of this are Albert Schweitzer, Mahatma Gandhi, and Martin Luther King. There must be some kind of contradiction going on here, and so reviewing the research makes it obvious that we must distinguish between two kinds of religious orientation, the extrinsic value and the intrinsic value. When we tested for these dimensions using a scale for extrinsicness and one for intrinsicness, lo and behold, we found that the extrinsic attitude is correlated with prejudice, and the intrinsic is correlated with very low prejudice. In other words, there is a curvilinear function with religion. I have to define extrinsic here as something that the person uses for his own purposes: to make friends, influence people, sell insurance, good times, prestige in the community, comfort, or wish fulfillment. He uses his religion in the same way that he uses his social groups and memberships. It's an exclusionistic point of view that can lead to prejudice because it is part of the fact that religion is solely for his benefit, and other people are not for his benefit. It's a very self-centered orientation and you would have to say a majority of people take their religion that way because the majority of churchgoers show this bigotry. On the other hand, there is a sizable minority whose attitude toward religion is quite the opposite; it plays an entirely different function for them because they serve it, it doesn't serve them. They have decided that the creeds and doctrines, including the doctrine of human brotherhood, are necessary for their value system, and they adopt for themselves the entire religious system, then live by it. It is not really valid to talk about the relationship of religion and prejudice in any gross way. Rather you've got to make a distinction between the two kinds of functions that religion can play in different personalities.

EVANS: And you are now attempting to isolate the two factors with further investigations?

ALLPORT: Yes. The word humanitarian, however, must be considered to be something much, much deeper than mere interest in fellow men. The trait I refer to is a genuine religiosity, a giving of oneself to his religion. Humanitarianism then becomes a by-product of it, but it is not considered to be "Humanitarian Religion." It is a religion which is not dependent on denominationalism; it is the way the person has taken the whole thing, and humanitarianism is the by-product of it.

EVANS: You're saying, then, that this intrinsic religion is a great deal more than a humanistic doctrine?

ALLPORT: You have to raise the question whether

humanism can be called a religion. It's a perfectly noble point of view that the best qualities in human beings should be cultivated, but that's not really religion. Religion includes the elements of wonder, mystery, and comprehensiveness in it; it's not just focused on human values, but way beyond them. I wouldn't agree that humanism is the same as religion. People raise the same question about communism, and wonder if it is a religion. I would say that it is not; it is certainly a way of life which represents a kind of functional substitute for religion, but it doesn't attempt to answer the questions that religion attempts to answer.

EVANS: Our culture pays a great deal of lip service to religiosity, but there seems to be underneath it all two strata of religious standards, one of which is voiced, and the other which is actually being practiced. This same kind of double standard applies to other areas of our culture; we talk about one kind of morality, but don't, in effect, carry it out. Theologians speak about religion as though it encompassed both the extrinsic and the intrinsic factors, but this variety seems to be on the wane. Do you feel that people are searching for different kinds of values now?

ALLPORT: It has often been said that society has become so secularized that religion has lost its hold, and I suppose there's some truth to that. On the other hand, churches seem to be attended just as much, and perhaps more, than they formerly were. This is not true in other countries as it is here where church attendance is high. But the motives may be mixed. I suspect that there is a lot of extrinsic motivation in our church attendance, so you couldn't infer from attendance that people are genuinely religious. My guess would be that over the ages you've always had just a minority of people who shelter a deep, comprehensive, pervasive intrinsic religious interest, and I'm not sure that the case is any different now than it's ever been.

EVANS: Because so many individuals put up a religious "front" or a facade by attending church, it makes the measurement of such a subtle personality characteristic as genuine religious sentiment rather difficult, does it not?

ALLPORT: I would advocate a much deeper psychological analysis of the role of religion in the life of the individual, not just the statistics.

EVANS: So you feel that the analyses we make of religion in our culture might be based on inadequate criteria or information based on inadequate judgment?

ALLPORT: Up to now, no adequate analysis has been made of the role religion plays in personality. I hope that I am making some little beginning on that.

EVANS: When we speak of religion in the life of the individual, it brings up a related question, the notion of maturity and its corollary, mental health. Our culture has set up such a standard of "good mental health" and "The Good Life" that Dr. Thomas Szasz has even been moved to write about the "myth of mental illness," in which he questions whether we may not have set up a false standard.

ALLPORT: The problem seems to revolve around ethics or value theory, and is a question that our philosophers have attempted to answer—What is the "Good Life"? I'm convinced, here, that a psychologist as a psychologist cannot answer that question, even though there are several ways in which he can contribute to the answer. Just to mention one, the psychologist can gather consensual judgments from a wide sample of people in an effort to define what is good or healthy or mature. Even a doctor can't define health, and I'm not sure that anyone can define maturity; it's a kind of ideal state that we think exists, but everyone sees it according to his own set of values. However, there is a lot of agreement on the subject, and I once wrote a paper attempting to summarize all the consensual studies that had been made. I prepared a chapter for my book, *Pattern and Growth in Personality* (8), drawing from Johada's study of positive mental health, and Barron's studies on sound personality, and some others. Briefly, we might give the example that the mature person will have interests outside his own immediate bodily needs; that is, he's not merely hedonistic. He must have some commitments or interests, or what I call ego extensions beyond his immediate bodily needs. He must have some kind of philosophy of life, such as an ideology or religion or commitment that will hold him together in times of trouble. He must also have a realistic perception of what's going on in the environment around him; he obviously can't have delusions, and so on. You could build up criteria of maturity, and that's what I did, but I don't think you can do it strictly on scientific psychological grounds. You must have a consensus of the ethical opinions of mankind, particularly those within your own culture.

EVANS: Some of your statements at the beginning of our discussion relative to your meeting with Sigmund Freud make me wonder to what degree Freud himself conceptualized an adequate standard of maturity and how psychoanalysis should proceed toward fulfilling it. Perhaps immaturity stems from a lack of something such as commitment, interest, ideology, or religion; so how, then, could psychoanalysis transmit this to the individual?

ALLPORT: When Freud was asked the question, "What should a healthy person do," the only thing I know of what he said about it was that the person should be able to love and to work. To my knowledge, these are the two criteria he held. They are good as far as they go, but I have already mentioned others, such as ego extension and philosophy of life, that I feel are equally essential to a condition of humanness. Freud's list of the requirements of maturity was a little bit sketchy.

EVANS: Do you feel that our culture really has a sufficiently concrete conception of maturity to pass on to its youth, so that values such as outside altruistic interests or ideology or commitment really are transmitted?

ALLPORT: Parents get a lot of blame and take a lot of the responsibility for child training as we discussed earlier, and, of course, the home is an important factor in the child's life relative to church and school. I suppose there are some parents who have goals in mind similar to the ones I mentioned and some parents don't. There are good parents and bad parents, and have been through the ages. I would say, however, that there is nothing predetermined about what values the child will acquire from its parents. I have known lives that had perfectly wretched starts: broken homes, cruelty, and sorrow, but that very fact somehow turned them to an entirely opposite philosophy of life in later years. They became determined that their own children would not suffer the same handicaps. It's one of the mysteries of personality, and you can't make a direct linear cause and effect relationship. Sometimes it fools you and reverses itself. But I suppose there would still be a statistical relation between the parents' own goals and the kind of personality youth develops, even though by no means a perfect correlation.

EVANS: It would be interesting to study groups of parents to find out to what degree they actually articulate or conceptualize the kinds of goals you have mentioned, and if possible learn the ways in which such goals are communicated to the children.

ALLPORT: There is a revealing study which comes to mind done by Harris, Gough, and Martin (6), who studied prejudice in children at the sixth grade level. When they found that some of the children were extremely prejudiced and some were not prejudiced, they asked the mothers of these children questions about child training practices. Without revealing their reasons for questioning the mothers, the investigators found a very significant difference between the philosophy of child training in the two groups. The prejudiced children had mothers who believed in firm punishment, who believed that the child should not talk back, who believed that the child should be whipped when he had tantrums, and so on; they were more authoritarian on the whole, and their children turned out to be more prejudiced. This is an example of studies on early attitude development, but there are not too many studies dealing with the relationship of child training practices to later attitudes.

EVANS: This question is a challenge to the whole mental health movement—what can the social psychologist communicate to society that will help that society be more mentally healthy? What advice can we give parents on issues such as child training or appropriate social values for them to pass along to the youth?

ALLPORT: Of course, we can't write a ticket—we don't know enough. But on the other hand, I am rather optimistic for the future because of the larger and larger numbers of young people who go to college, where they encounter new insights and attain some objectivity about the matter of mental health. Most of it is acquired through reading and discussion, and even there they find no rule-of-thumb formula. I hope they don't acquire a set rule because I don't think it's a safe course to follow, but through general wisdom or enlightenment, I hope that the next generation will be better for it.

EVANS: Your statement implies that you have faith in the intellectual enlightenment acquired at the college level being effective in overcoming the effects of early training. Your view diverges here somewhat from psychoanalytic thinkers who argue that intellectuality doesn't effectively transcend the emotional fixations of early life.

ALLPORT: I think the point at which I disagree most with psychoanalysis, as I suggested earlier in our discussion, is when it claims that the guidelines of character are laid down by the age of three or four. I think that's pretty much nonsense. In some cases you find a neurosis which can be traced to some early cause, but in the normal personality it isn't true at all. On the other hand, I don't want to overstress the value of simple intellectual information or book education. I know that of itself intellectualization does not change attitudes, emotions, or values too much, but in the long run, it's bound to percolate through the personality and have some effect.

EVANS: Another area of current and continuing interest in psychology is the area of personality testing and measurement, in that it seems to imply a nomothetic approach where the tester looks for common traits, as you call them. In order adequately to understand the individual, one must use phenotypical (descriptive) information, and yet at the same time know that it doesn't do adequate justice to the individual. Is there a means by which we can handle this dilemma?

ALLPORT: Yes, I've worked on that problem, and I think that I have the proper direction to look for an answer. We've simply neglected the study of personal dispositions which I think can be done purely quantitatively. For example, when Cantril asks people to define the best possible way of life for themselves and the worst possible way, then he puts those on a ladder of ten rungs. Then he asks the people where they stand now, where five years ago, and where they expect to stand two years from now. This gives him a morphogenic anchorage point, and indicates their best possible way of life. It's more than just a common trait. But you can do a good deal of quantifying within this morphogenic concept because it represents a self-anchoring scale. Another example is the case of personal documents which represents strictly morphogenic material. I have some very fascinating material called *Letters from Jenny* (9) which one of my former students, Professor Al Baldwin, used in a course to count the relationship of ideas in Jenny's mind. This would not be nomothetic because it didn't involve any other person but Jenny. But if Jenny talked about her son, he noted what else she talked about in the same paragraph or thought sequence. Because this method exposes the thought structure of her mind, it isn't a common trait approach, you see. I don't agree, therefore, that all measurement must be nomothetic. I think we can go much farther than we have in discovering ways of constructing the actual personal dispositions of individuals even in a quantitative way. That is a pertinent problem in the use of projective methods. I think that for the most part they're handled in a strictly nomothetic way— that is, you have so much f-plus sign or so much M, and therefore the diagnostic indications are that so and so is true across the board. As you say, it's really a common trait approach, but there are clinicians who claim to use it more clinically by looking at the variables for a pattern trend and going on from there. The approaches used by people like Dr. Magda Arnold with the Thematic Apperception Test try to get at personal characteristics through a fairy-story sequence which serves as a diagnostic indicator, but is not scored routinely according to an established pattern of responses. These are problems which have not yet been adequately resolved.

EVANS: Some people have suggested that this projective testing emphasizes the unconscious unduly making it difficult to validate them properly. Do you feel there is a legitimate place for them in psychological research?

ALLPORT: Yes, I certainly do feel they have a place. What I've said about them is that they should never be used without also using direct methods. If a person, for example, is consciously and unconsciously anxious, it means something very different from when he's only unconsciously anxious. How are you going to know that you're tapping the unconscious unless you know also what is conscious? I think I would be dogmatic and say that we should never use projective tests unless we also use direct methods of interview or pencil-and-paper tests in order to make comparisons between them. I don't think you've diagnosed the personality as a whole by using only the projective-test method.

EVANS: Would you feel this way also about the use of dream interpretations?

ALLPORT: Yes, I think so.

EVANS: Do you feel that our extreme concern with measurement might lead us to a kind of sterility in our thinking concerning personality?

ALLPORT: There is no doubt that many psychologists have an overconcern for measurement, and I think it's most regrettable. It's a tool, but if it makes one think that one has embraced the totality of a personality by having a series of scores, then it has gone too far. The problem is in the way scores interact with each other. Each person has within himself a distinctive pattern of interaction, and no amount of mere measurement will tell you what it is.

EVANS: Were you attempting to get at this kind of thing by using the psychograph to yield a profile of scores?

ALLPORT: Even this profile doesn't show an interaction. A psychograph or a profile is the very essence of what comes out of measurements. You plot a point here and plot a point there, and it doesn't tell you what interaction there is between them. You don't learn what high intelligence has to do with his submissiveness; this can't be inferred from the profile. You would have to deal directly with the person to learn how the two interact, and what the individual pattern really is.

EVANS: You are saying, then, that even the psychograph or record of a battery of test scores does injustice to the individual.

ALLPORT: It does not relate his parts to each other. These measures don't relate his lungs to his other parts; they relate his lungs to other peoples' lungs.

EVANS: Carl Jung (12) was particularly proud of his word-association method of testing, and in a sense he might be considered a pioneer of projective methods. Then Rorschach developed a more complex method by which he was able to make broader inferences concerning personality to which you alluded earlier. I wonder how you feel about the possibility of using words and language more directly to arrive at personality measurements?

ALLPORT: There are fashions and fashions in psychology; we never solve a problem, we just grow tired of it. I think we can see that this happens. In the 1910–1930 era, the Jung method of word association was based on standards of English usage developed by several psychologists in this country. It was fairly widely used, and in fact it still is the basis for lie-detection work. Then we went into sentence completion and other fashions like multiple scales which yielded a multiple scale composed of several traits at one sitting. Presently this method is rather neglected. It's a sound theory to assume that the first word which comes to mind after a stimulus word is presented has been filtered through a lot of the structures of your personality and would be a valid indication of your selective process in terms of personality structure. I think it's a sound method, and should be developed and employed.

EVANS: That's an interesting observation you made about fashions. You are saying that techniques of measurement shift sometimes more because of superficial reasons than because they actually yield more valid and penetrating analyses of personality.

ALLPORT: Yes, I'm sure that some of the changes are quite accidental. A teacher will be interested in a particular method for a while and will have students who become excited about it, and they keep each other interested for a while, but then they both tire of it or something else comes along and a new method evolves. These risings and fallings of fashion do lose us some very penetrating work because they are dropped before they become fully developed. It's for this reason that I insist my students be as well grounded historically as they can so that they will know when they lay aside one method that they have given it a fair trial, and not because fashion has dictated a change.

EVANS: Incidentally, we couldn't engage in a discussion of personality measurement without pursuing further the significant personality measure which you yourself have developed along with Professors Vernon and Lindzey, the Study of Values. It seems to have never gone out of fashion. It's another example of the use of ostensibly nomothetic measurement designed to get at individuality, is it not?

ALLPORT: That particular instrument is a curious hybrid. My colleague, Professor Marsteller, in statistics, tells me that there is no such scale possible. But it has been used for some thirty years or more and so there you have it. Actually, that instrument stands halfway between dimensional and morphogenic methods in a curious respect, and this is what probably bothers Professor Marsteller. There are, at the outset, six common traits: the theoretical, aesthetic, social, political, religious, and economic. These were defined by Spranger (24) originally, and our test invites you to indicate the relative strength of these six values in your own personality. Consequently, your score cannot be compared with anyone else's because the test reflects relative strengths of those values within your own personality. Conceivably, a person whose aesthetic value was the lowest of his six might still be more aesthetic than a person whose highest value was aesthetic because he might have a lot of values or express a lot of value energy. He might also be so apathetic about life that he doesn't appear to have any values at all as measured by the test, so his scores cannot be compared with other persons. They are only relevant to the person who takes it. We begin, therefore, with an instrument which measures six common traits, but end with a profile that is strictly personal and individual.

EVANS: It must have been interesting for you to find that the Study of Values scale, after being unnoticed for awhile, suddenly emerged as a significant experimental tool in studies of selective perception.

ALLPORT: I was surprised and gratified by its effectiveness, but in a way, also anticipated this result because it has always been my theory that the high level organizations, such as values, are gaiting mechanisms through which perceptions, responses, and attention emerge. Since this is my theory, it was not too surprising that the test demonstrated itself to be a useful tool in screening people who would have selective attention, selective reactions, selective prejudices, according to these values. I wasn't surprised at that even though the test was not intended for that kind of research. I'm very gratified, however, that it has been useful and has established an important theoretical fact, namely that higher-level attitudes and values do serve as gaiting mechanisms for specific perceptions and reactions and judgments.

EVANS: Another area of continuing interest in psychology is the best approach to the training of psychology students. We run into the question of breadth versus narrowness of curriculum. In terms of a proper course of development of the student, should he be trained to become open-minded and eclectic, or should he adopt a well-defined point of view in psychology and become expert in that?

ALLPORT: All during my thirty years' experience teaching students, I've been concerned about the proper diet for young graduate psychology students; and the same is true for undergraduates, as well. There is a lot to be said on both sides, both in favor of the narrow, specialist-expert training and for the broader scope. On the side of specializing, it can be said that one learns scientific methodology and is trained in dealing with close thinking on hard-nosed problems. Furthermore, I feel that unless you've got something to react against, you don't grow up. If you get firmly set in a belief, then find out five years later that what you believed just doesn't cover the problem you're dealing with, then you have something to react against, and you can go on to wider horizons, knowing the weaknesses of the methods already tried. So there is something to be said for narrow, specialist training at the graduate level; but I don't think it has to be all or none. I'm afraid most people get their habits set and never broaden their horizons later. The formula we at Harvard have attempted to work out is to require social psychology students to know something of the physiological, biological, sociological, and anthropological side of the story. This kind of diet includes both the biotropic and the sociotropic reference points, and students then become specialists in some research field of their own interest ranging between these two extremes. In addition, they must pass examinations in a history of psychology, and the background of theories and systems. We're attempting to ride two horses at once: the steed of specialization, and the steed of interdisciplinary breadth, and it's difficult to do. Students sometimes rebel, and often would like the narrower drill-type curriculum, which is reflected in the fact that they often do their theses on extremely narrow, limited subjects. We try to be permissive about it, and we accept this work, but my own view is to give them sufficient breadth so that they can come back to the specialization later. All psychology rests on philosophical presuppositions of some sort, and I think students should realize that and know enough about those presuppositions so that if one approach proves less fruitful than the student anticipated, he can turn to another.

EVANS: The term "scientism" was coined some years ago by Professor Hayek, who, of course, was being sarcastic, but it points to the extreme degree to which psychology in particular seems to be obsessed with the scientific frame of reference as we discussed earlier in another context. This charge may or may not be true, but if it is, we might ask why is it so important to emphasize scientific methodology.

ALLPORT: The extreme position which you identified has also been called methodolatry, and I think it's important to distinguish between being method-centered and being problem-centered. I certainly have no objections to precise methods, and we require of all our students training in advanced statistics, for example. But when it comes to building a whole lifetime around method and worshipping a certain narrow conception of precision, I think that is not helpful. Originally, science meant knowledge; the Latin word "scientia" simply means knowledge, and the German word for science "Wissenschaft" has the same broad meaning, knowledge. I'm not willing to call our more loosely conceived work on broader problems unscientific; the work centers on the problems at hand, and we use the methods we have. There are many method-worshippers in psychology, and I think it's unfortunate because they don't have much sense of the nature of the problem. Our journals show a preponderance of small bits of empirical studies, elegantly designed methodologically, but having little bearing on the problems which originated the research. It seems to me that we should have a better balance between our instruction and our outlook on the matter of suitable methods for important problems, but without losing sight of the problems themselves.

EVANS: The psychologist is increasingly being faced with the responsibility of doing evaluative research on society's efforts to solve significant human problems such as poverty, racial desegregation, overpopulation, or environmental pollution. Such research can seldom be very rigorous. Do you feel that such less-than-rigorous research efforts, which are often merely thoughtful approximations, can really contribute to psychology?

ALLPORT: Yes, such thoughtful approximations can and have done much to advance our knowledge in psychology. In studies on attitude change, for example, some cross-cultural studies have been done. The question was what changes come about as a result of students spending a summer in Europe; what does it do to their outlook, attitudes, prejudices, and information. You can give them a test before they go and again after they return, and you can attempt to have a control group, but that's a difficult aspect of the problem. The social psychologist is familiar with the scientific precautions, and he attempts to make allowances for them. Our questions are loosely phrased, our instruments are open-ended, and the questions are easily misunderstood, even though every precaution is taken to make them perfect. A typical example of the issues social psychology must investigate was on an experiment in international living sponsored by American Friends Volunteer Service Work Camps on the Cross-roads to Africa. The problem was to do a social policy evaluation of the experiment. It is a big policy and it certainly should be evaluated, else how do we know that they're worth the effort and time? So the social psychologist knows scientific standards and then uses the best methods he can. With this, he comes as near as he can to good research and the results are always interesting and sometimes very helpful. Through them, policies are sometimes shaped or revised.

EVANS: Some of our more rigorous methodologists frequently condemn this kind of research. It tends to put the graduate student in social psychology on the defensive, as though he were fighting for a kind of respectability. The internal establishment in psychology has set up rigorous research methodology as the guiding standard. The student who deals with a social research problem more complex than can be implemented this rigorously becomes defensive about it or may be encouraged to abandon it altogether. Have you any words of comfort to the student facing such a dissertation problem?

ALLPORT: This point presses us pretty hard. I could be rather sharp and say that childish concern for an idol of the academy is unworthy of the mature person; that the student should follow his own values and his own sense of appropriateness, and do the best he can. This kowtowing to intolerance is personally quite intolerable. That's a sharp answer, and to it I must add that I have no objection to a student being well trained in method. But why, just because he's young, should he accept someone else's idol for his life goal when his own interests tell him he might do something more daring and imaginative? I don't see it. A good many students grow out of the stage of wanting respectability. Of course, the young student is insecure—he's got to see where the so-called rewards lie. It surprises me, though, that you feel this is a widespread problem. We don't see it much here because we don't lead our students into worship of method for its own sake, and most of my colleagues are people of some cultivation and breadth. It's rather a minority who try to impose this rigid conception that a given formula is all that is acceptable in science. I don't feel that way about it and I think very, very few mature teachers do either.

EVANS: In his 1951 book on *Personality*, your colleague, David McClelland (19), personified you as one of three types of investigators in personality psychology. His discussion dealt with the problem of objectivity that the personality theorist faces because the study of personality involves studying the self. He suggested that a type of self-insulation is sought by the psychologist to maintain objectivity. He illustrated how Freud protected himself against subjectivity by a kind of cynicism. He saw man as basically an animal. Behaviorists attempt to avoid subjectivity by focusing on the response of the individual and dealing as little with the experience of the individual as possible. McClelland postulates still another kind of approach which has its basis in a positive attitude toward man and reflects a basic optimism. He feels that you represent the approach which holds an appreciative positive, optimistic attitude toward man. He raises the question whether such a positive attitude toward man doesn't place the psychologist more in the realm of artist rather than scientist, since this doesn't avoid subjectivity in the psychologists' inquiry into the nature of man.

ALLPORT: Well, with apologies to my colleague Dave McClelland, I would like to answer "fiddlesticks." He seems to be representing the position of psychologism, which is essentially that there is no basic science except psychology; there is no standard of truth except your own subjective temperament, and what you like. If you write a book on personality, you are likely to project your own personality into it, and if you're softheaded, your theory will be softheaded, and so on. That is a logically impossible point of view because it commits the fallacy of saying that everybody except you is subjective, relativistic, projective, but that you are making a judgment which is absolutely correct and profound. McClelland seems to be there setting himself up in a position to judge everyone else as being subjective; but his generalization is correct. I would turn the tables on him and say, "What is it in your temperament and your personality that makes you make such an absolute judge about the psychological relativity of everyone else's judgment?" It's really an impossible position from a logical point of view. You've got to assume that there is objective truth. I don't know what sort of personality I have; I don't care, and I don't think it's relevant. I have to put into my books my best judgment about the nature of human beings according to the best evidence that I have been able to accumulate. Much of it is scientific evidence; some of it not so scientific in method, but I don't think it should be left out. I don't believe it's a projection of my own temperament or emotion; it's the best I can do objectively. It may be wrong but it can be tested on objective grounds without a battle of personalities being involved.

EVANS: Dr. McClelland was advocating the Socratic conception of "let the truth be known" by saying that we shouldn't purchase neutrality at the cost of ignoring certain problems. He raised this criticism against the behaviorists by suggesting that they confine themselves to the narrow observable facets of the individual and avoid the issues which are not readily observable, thereby relieving themselves of the necessity of looking too carefully at the "O" or the individual organism. He feels that each of these three positions has its unique problems, and the scientist must be guided by the "let the truth be known wherever it falls" attitude. You've indicated essentially the same position.

ALLPORT: Yes, this would involve the aspects of neutrality, and I'm all for it. But I might claim that it can be achieved much more readily than McClelland implies. I don't care what motivated Freud, Hull, Dollard, Miller, or Skinner. It seems to me that their ideas can be tested on objective grounds and either be accepted or not accepted according to a bulk of evidence. Truth is, I think, what informed people are eventually fated to agree upon.

EVANS: Ernest Jones in his dialogue with me (12) was a little upset by the criticism of Freud which suggested that a good deal of Freud's work was an acting-out of his own personality and that his system was surely a reflection of his own life history. You're agreeing that such a judgment about Freud would be completely irrelevant. We should merely be guided by what Freud said, then evaluate it.

ALLPORT: Yes. I don't care what his motivation was; what he said was right or wrong, and it must be judged on that ground only. I'm not denying, of course, that there is a projectivity in our thought, and it often leads us to falsehoods if we merely project our own desires and emotions. But these will be discovered sooner or later, and the residual truth will remain.

EVANS: You mentioned being an academic psychologist, Dr. Allport, and I wonder if you would elaborate what you mean by that. A label such as this does not always have the same meaning to people, and I wonder if you are implying that to be academic one would, among other things, not engage in clinical activity. Would there be advantages to the student, for instance, to remain an academic psychologist rather than become engaged in clinical practice?

ALLPORT: I think clinical experience would be very good for any psychologist, even though I must admit I'm not a psychotherapist or a consulting psychologist myself. I did have some experience in social work at one time. I have nothing against a background of clinical experience or training; it would actually be valuable to have more than I have had. But I consider myself to be academic in the sense that I've always spent my time in universities. I believe that one dealing with concepts and attitudes must study the historical development and use books to a large extent to follow up that history. I'm afraid the modern generation doesn't keep up with research as much as it should. I've tried to build on everything of the past that I found to be valid and sound and have attempted to get it organized into a system. I don't claim to have done it, but I think I have opened avenues to the study of personality that may lead to the right one. Personality itself is an open system, and being open must refer to the culture out of which it develops, to changing philosophies of life, and to make allowances for man's capability and potentiality. There are criteria which distinguish an open system and I have written about them, but I have just given the rough answer that if you take personality as an open system, then the facts can be fitted in from many systems or points of view, and the result will be something reasonably systematic. Some people will argue that systematic eclecticism is a contradiction in terms, but I don't think it necessarily is, as I implied earlier in our discussion.

EVANS: You mentioned the criteria for an open system, but an example of a system which has been closed by some is psychoanalytic theory. Do you feel that Freud's work reflected a closed system in terms of your interpretation of closed system?

ALLPORT: I would say that Freud's psychoanalytic system was never really closed. When I define closed system, I rely on biological terminology and say that there is no closed system excepting a stone or an old barn. Something which obeys the second law of thermodynamics and falls to pieces would be closed. But a system which is self-reconstituting, or has dynamic growth potential, is technically an open system. Ultimately it's all a matter of degree. Freud's system would be called quasi-closed because he allows, at least in his earlier writings, for input and output of energy and for homeostasis. He described the ego attempting to maintain equilibrium between the tyrants of the id and the superego and the external world. That is essentially a homeostatic theory which I could call semiclosed because it does not allow for continuous differentiation or growth from within the organism over time. My criterion for a really open system would include a dynamic growth process as well as interactional elements between the organism and its environment. Later Freudian thought, or neo-Freudian, includes much more of the third criterion, which is that the ego itself is dynamic; it has a goal and interest system in its own right—what Hartman calls a secondary autonomy—and that comes close to some of my own views about the nature of personality.

EVANS: As you have used these concepts to expand your earlier observations, would you say there is a real distinction between the systematized eclecticism to which you just referred and an integrative or synthesized approach?

ALLPORT: No, I don't think so. In either case you have a framework, and I'm merely suggesting that the framework and conceptions characterizing an open system would allow room to include other things you observe. It would allow for everything that isn't closed. The knee jerk, the automatic behavioral responses, and the simple learning of rewarded responses would be essentially consistent with a semiclosed theory of personality. Insofar as it is valid, all this can be lumped into the open personality system without excluding those elements which go beyond the semiclosed functions. There is room within an open system for both extremes, and that's why it's more comprehensive, and, to me, more acceptable.

EVANS: Holding valid, as you do, the notion of systematic eclecticism, you must have run into the criticism that the more open the system, the less it lends itself to the utilization of rigorous research methodology.

ALLPORT: I would almost have to repeat what I have said earlier in that problems dealing with attitude and prejudice, religious sentiment, and attitude changes are all open systems, and must be considered to be valid fields for research even though the methodology may not be as rigorous as for more closed systems.

EVANS: You are implying, then, that for practical purposes, closed systems tend to breed preoccupation with methodology and open systems allow for broader areas of research?

ALLPORT: Yes, the open system invites imagination for the invention of new methods which can be as rigorous as possible, but not to the extent of surrendering your problem.

EVANS: Referring back to a notion we discussed before, that the work of a person often reflects his own personality organization, could we project this into the areas of creativity in general and really separate the creative effort of an individual from his personality? To what degree would you say the artistic effort of the artist could reveal significant understanding of the artist?

ALLPORT: Art, of course, is highly expressive; it invites maximum use of the personality and particularly the subjective and unconscious aspects of it. I feel, therefore, that one can see a little more clearly in an artistic production the expressive side of the personality. But I would say that such an evaluation has nothing to do with the aesthetic merit of the production. Judgments about personality and artistic value of the work are two separate aspects of the problem.

EVANS: This brings us back to a consideration of your research using autobiographical material in attempting to learn how personality patterns develop within an individual. Do you feel that this will be a productive area of research into dynamics of personality development?

ALLPORT: I feel that the area of research could be productive, and my colleague, Anne Roe, using autobiographical data, has tried to make some generalizations about personalities of natural scientists as differentiated from psychological scientists. Some of her findings are quite interesting. My interest in autobiographical materials, however, has been centered more on individual developmental patterns than an attempt to generalize over a variety of types of vocational choices. My primary concern was to learn what value diaries, letters, and autobiographies might be in the study of personality. I wrote a monograph dealing with *The Use of Personal Documents in Psychological Science* (3), and I considered in it the problems of reliability and validity of interpretation using such materials. As we discussed earlier, I'm presently working on theories relevant to the use of *Letters from Jenny* (9) which I hope to edit and issue in a paperback book in order to show how much value one can find in personal documents relevant to the study of the single life pattern. It's not an effort to learn what particular kind of pattern evolves out of such a study, but to see how much of value we can learn from studying good material that is a valid interpretation of a single life sequence.

EVANS: You're saying, then, that you are attempting to get a full picture of the individual through the study of autobiographical material, whereas the other approach is to use such material merely to generate predictions about vocational choices.

ALLPORT: This, in fact, touches on a point where a good many people disagree with me, and for which I have been held up as an example of near-romanticism. I believe that all science can and should work to understand the pattern of an individual life. I believe that the one is unique, never repeated, and never existent before. Each individual life is unique and worthy of itself to be studied for its uniqueness. On the other hand, I do not advocate an exclusively morphogenic or idiographic approach. I'm interested in the mind in general, but my point is that we need new methods and better methods to study this enormously intricate pattern that is the individual.

THREATS TO MAN AND SOCIETY; EVALUATIONS OF MOST SIGNIFICANT CONTRIBUTIONS; THE FUTURE OF PERSONALITY PSYCHOLOGY

PART IV

Man and Overconformity

Psychologists' Role in Solving Social Problems

Psychologists and World Peace

Estimate of His Own Most Important Contributions

The Future of Personality Psychology

Overview | In this section I present to Dr. Allport questions relating to man and society, among them the problem of overconformity of man in this highly technological society, the role of the psychologist in solving significantly threatening problems such as nuclear war, and man's struggle for world peace. I also solicit his estimates of what he considers the most significant among his contributions, and finally obtain his judgment as to what he believes the future of personality psychology will be.

EVANS: To move to still another area, Dr. Allport, a formidable body of social critics sees us developing into a nation of overconformists, where individuality, as such, is completely lost. Otto Rank spoke of the average man; Erich Fromm speaks of the marketing orientation which swallows the individual in the system; and David Riesman writes of the other-directed man. These men see our culture as producing men who learn to get ahead by playing the game, by conforming to the degree that their very individuality is increasingly eradicated. Do you share this somewhat pessimistic view of our cultural trend?

ALLPORT: I don't doubt that there is some truth in these charges. Gamesmanship along with automation and bureaucratization of life tend to detract one from a personal development and leave the individual just able to get by if he joins the crowd and becomes an organization man. There is certainly some truth in the allegation, but it's awfully easy to make types representing inner-directedness or outer-directedness. I'm inclined to think that the challenge to the healthy person is to learn to play the game where necessary, to meet the requirements of the culture, and still to have integrity, to maintain some self-objectification, and not to lose his personal values and commitments. It becomes more and more difficult to do, but I believe it can be done. It implies that the personality of the future will operate under more of a strain, but we don't yet know what the actual potentiality of human development can be. We may be able to eat our cake and have it too by playing the organization game while remaining the individual of integrity and personal commitment.

EVANS:　You're saying that a reasonable amount of adaptation may be necessary, but need not necessarily endanger individuality.

ALLPORT:　Yes, that's what I'm trying to say.

EVANS:　Ernest Jones in his dialogue with me (12) made an interesting comment relevant to conformity when he suggested that we are actually becoming more and more individualistic rather than conforming, because of the very fact that we're so preoccupied with conformity. He feels that awareness of it tends to reduce its strength as a potential danger to the individual.

ALLPORT:　I have to agree that students in this generation are worried about conformity. I think it's a very healthy sign, and as long as they continue to worry about it, I shan't worry.

EVANS:　A question related to a slightly different area of human relations stems from the threat of nuclear war. Julian Huxley a few years ago drew the analogy between the vast technological developments capable of destroying the world and our substantially less-developed ability to understand human relations. He felt that we have developed the ability to destroy ourselves without the ability to understand and control the impulses which would lead us to do it. Do you feel the situation is as bad as Huxley indicates, or might there be something we as psychologists could do about it?

ALLPORT: It's a profound question, and it's also true that we have learned to master interstellar space without having learned much about our own inner space. Inside the skull, the brain weighs about two pounds, and we know less about it than we do about sputniks and satellites. I think it's the paradox of human development that we are very much out of phase. And to answer what we might be able to do about it, I can only point to two relevant considerations. One is that the expenditure for interstellar space research is many hundreds of times greater than expenditures for psychological and sociological research. It seems to me to be more than a matter of money—psychological and sociological sciences are intrinsically vastly more difficult than physics or chemistry, no matter how difficult they appear to be. We have a more difficult problem requiring much more subtle techniques, and we aren't giving proportionate time to it. That's one line of thought. We could step up our work in the social sciences, and it might help some. But I also think that since the character of an individual person is really at the root of behavior and wisdom, our statesmen and policymakers must make more allowances for the individual personality to allow for its creativity, imagination, and moral growth. Social science can help a good deal in educating parents through college courses, but in the last analysis, it's up to the individual person to contribute what he can, to know his own duties in this crisis facing the human race. There is a very personal aspect to this problem. I can't just say, "Leave it to the churches," because they've been working on it for 2,000 years, and haven't had much success in improving human morality and peace on earth. I certainly would not interfere with what the churches are doing, but I think we've got to find ways of appealing to people for their own individual responsibility. These are the world's needs, not merely one's own loyalties, but a much larger conception.

EVANS: Getting back again to our discussion of the value of the psychologist doing rigorous research, as against doing approximate evaluations when we deal with important complex human problems, the very role of the behavioral scientist seems to come into question if we probe more deeply into this issue beyond seeing the behavioral scientist as a researcher. Even within our profession there is a difference of opinion about what that role should be, some feeling that the social or behavioral scientist must engage himself solely in the understanding, describing, and predicting of behavior, while others feel that he should enter the mainstream of society and take an active role in changing society. It gets to be a tricky problem since as we discussed earlier some define "respectability" of the behavioral scientist in terms of the neutral observer stance. How do you feel about this matter?

ALLPORT: You're referring to those who advocate basic research regardless of its applicability to anything. It reminds me of the foundation executive who asked an applicant seeking funds, "Now, is this basic research, or do you have something in mind?" My view is that I certainly would not curtail basic research and we definitely need that. There are people, fortunately, who by temperament continue to work along at a problem regardless of its consequences or its application, and we need that kind of perseverence. There are also the social scientists who engage in what we call action research, dealing with prejudice, attitude change, and evaluation of television programs. Their research is equally good science; they certainly have no interest in fooling themselves so they don't overgeneralize their results. It's good honest research. But to each of these scientists, I say that they have responsibilities as citizens, and as such certain duties in the matter of world affairs. They can, without interfering the least bit with the validity of their scientific work, become partisan and express their values and work within the framework of democracy for the improvement of society.

EVANS: This brings us back to the question of the role of the social scientist in society. Obviously, he can, as a citizen, espouse any system of values or ideological position he chooses. On the other hand, when he steps into society in his role as a social scientist, he is seen as having a special status, and his opinion then takes on the aspect of "expertise." When you refer to the scientist taking social responsibility, do you mean as a private citizen or by bringing his expertness to bear directly on social problems?

ALLPORT: Both, in a sense. It seems to me that his motivation to be a citizen and play his part is a personal one, and not in itself necessarily scientific expertise. But he certainly would use what wisdom he has acquired from his science whenever he offers his opinion. I hope that social scientists will be modest about their opinions, at least for a long time to come. He can say, "Well, of course, we can't solve this particular problem, but the best evidence I have after thirty years (or whatever it is) of experience is that such-and-such a policy would result in the most favorable consequences." In this way, the scientist can be both expert and citizen without really violating a scientific conscience.

EVANS: As scientists begin lending their expert opinions to the solution of social problems, we frequently run into the difficulty of divergences of judgment among them. We sometimes have as much expert judgment in support of one course of action as we have in support of the opposite course of action, and the difficulty could become intensified as more behavioral scientists move into society. It happened in the case of child-rearing patterns concerning the discipline-permissive problem, for example. It's probably not a fair question since there may be no simple answer, but do you feel that there might be a way to resolve such a conflict?

ALLPORT: I would say that it goes back to the matter of modesty. It's ridiculous to see two experts pounding a table on exactly opposite sides of an issue, each claiming to have absolute truth. It's obvious that they don't both have absolute scientific truth, or they'd agree on it. I think if the scientist is modest about the matter and says, "Well, so far as my ability goes, this is my best judgment," then if a social scientist crops up with the opposite judgment, well, let the jury or the outsider weigh the two positions and see which is most viable. The entire behavioral science field is really an infant science and I don't think we can pretend to solve the problems of the world at this point. But, on the other hand, I don't see why we shouldn't contribute what wisdom we have and let others judge its value.

EVANS: A popular area of involvement for the behavioral scientist is what we call peace research. This term has acquired certain stereotyped perceptions because it has sometimes been used as a front for a variety of other behind-the-scenes political activities, but do you feel that it is possible to address psychological research to such profound problems?

ALLPORT: It's an example of an enormously acute problem where the knowledge and ability of science to make a meaningful contribution is slight. For one thing, it's a relatively new problem, but since nothing in the world is more important than maintaining peace, scientists certainly should do what they can to solve it. They will have to begin at scratch because the factors contributing to the problem are unknown; we know some of them, but they are extremely complicated. They involve personalities of leaders, history, economics, politics, the limits of human intelligence, and prejudices. All kinds of factors enter into that situation and we must begin somewhere. Those of my colleagues who are trying to open doors or make little cracks in the walls of international hostility should be assisted in every way possible. Some of the thoughts so far produced on the matter seem to be quite suggestive. For example, Osgood's work (19) on reciprocal withdrawal is sound scientific work, and could easily be made into a national or international policy. The problem here is the gap between intelligent insight and operational functioning. Social scientists can contribute to some degree, but the policy-makers either don't know about their work or distrust it, and sometimes justifiably, but they don't quite know what to do with such contributions. It sums up to the fact that we must first build a better bridge between intelligence and operations.

EVANS: Another incidental problem that comes up when the social scientist becomes involved with action agencies is that he sometimes becomes acculturated to the agency's bureaucratic operation and loses his identity as a psychologist. For example, a psychologist working for the State Department may easily become so involved in the day-to-day activities of the Department that he no longer functions as a psychologist. He seems to have something special to offer only when he first enters this agency and clearly is perceived as and sees himself primarily as a psychologist, or sociologist, or cultural anthropologist and functions in this role.

ALLPORT: Yet it seems to me that we do need a kind of middleman, who can identify with the problems of an agency as well as with the problems of the policymaker. He should carry with him some knowledge, and if he keeps abreast of his specialty and is willing to deal with agency problems, he could be a very valuable bridge. But, as you say, some do lose their identity entirely, and perhaps some others might remain such ivory-tower scientists that they really have little to offer. I was talking with a man from the State Department just the other day who raised this same question. He asked, "What can you social scientists contribute to our very great international problems, such as developing underdeveloped countries, and so on?" I answered him, "I'm not sure that we've got anything to contribute, but I'm furious with you for not using it." He laughed and said, "I feel the same way. I feel that you fellows must have something to contribute, and that we ought to use it, but I don't know where to begin." In a case like this, we might very well put a social scientist into the operation and let him try to be the intermediary that is greatly needed. You will notice that I'm not saying social science has the answers, but I do think that we've got something to contribute to many policies and decisions.

EVANS: In a still different vein, Dr. Allport, I wonder if you would be willing to share with us your feelings concerning which of the contributions you have made to psychology *you* feel to be the most significant.

ALLPORT: It seems odd, perhaps, but I have never thought about this matter at all. All my work has focused on personality theory, particularly on the structure and the motivation of the personality. From that, I moved into the field of prejudice as a side line, to the individual and his religion, to the field of attitudes, personal documents, and expressive behavior. Everything has been focused around the central question of the nature of the human being and has been essentially a philosophical question. I have attempted to get reasoned empirical answers that shed some light on the issue, and they have come from different directions. I'm not sure which one thing I would point to as a significant contribution, but I feel that perhaps my early work on expressive behavior was somewhat overlooked. I, myself, dropped active research in that field, but I still feel that it would be important for us to understand how such factors as facial expression, posture, gait, gestures, and handwriting can reveal the innermost parts of the personality. We'd be a lot wiser if we knew more about it, but that's a problem for the future because there is not a great deal of research to report. The first published monograph, *Studies in Expressive Movement* (10), which I did with P. E. Vernon, I think I would point to as something which will be significant in the future.

EVANS: Could we ask you to speculate a bit here on the future of personality psychology? There are some who would even eliminate the use of the term personality because they see it as too vague, ill-defined, and diffuse to deal with in truly scientific terms.

ALLPORT: That's rather asking me to be a prophet, isn't it? I don't feel any more competent than anyone else to prophesy, but I suspect that psychology will expand in both directions. After all, there are 30,000 members in the American Psychological Association, and there will be all types of psychologists. We need all types too, and I just hope that they will be tolerant of each other. I do feel that there is a strong movement now away from the exclusively narrow methodolatry because of the influence of journals like *Individual Psychology, Humanistic Psychology, Existential Psychology,* as well as the development of the Association for Humanistic Psychology and the impact of the existential movement in its various forms. I'm quite certain there will be a strong movement toward what is called a third force which will be neither behavioristic nor psychoanalytic. But I wouldn't be willing to predict that it will dominate the field, though I can say I do hope it will develop sturdily and result in fruitful new methods to approach molar and complex levels of personality structure and social behavior.

EVANS: You're saying that you see a kind of psychology emerging which will integrate elements of behaviorism with the study of human personality.

ALLPORT: There will be a place for all types. Human nature is such a hard nut to crack that no one should be denied a chance to contribute to it at any level.

EVANS: Do you feel there may be such a breach among psychologists that, the strictly behavioristically oriented group might completely disassociate themselves from psychology as a whole?

ALLPORT: Separatism of that sort would be natural under the circumstances, but I personally hope it won't happen because we need each other, and we need as much communication as we can establish between the different types of psychologists.

EVANS: Dr. Allport, it has been a real pleasure to be with you here in your study where so many of the publications we've discussed were prepared. I particularly appreciate your willingness to participate in this dialogue and feel that it has been most enlighten: ing for our students, as well as for myself, to meet you as "the whole person." It's been a marvelous experience, and I've enjoyed being here with you.

ALLPORT: Your questions have not always been easy, but it has been fun to have a try at them.

SYMPOSIUM: "GORDON ALLPORT: HIS UNIQUE CONTRIBUTIONS TO CONTEMPORARY PERSONALITY AND SOCIAL PSYCHOLOGY"

PART V

Overview | In September 1969, approximately two years after Dr. Allport's untimely death, I had the privilege of chairing a symposium at the annual meeting of the American Psychological Association held in Washington, D.C., under the auspices of its Division of Personality and Social Psychology.

Three distinguished psychologists who had studied under Dr. Allport at Harvard participated in the discussion which followed a screening of some of the filmed portion of the dialogue. The content of the symposium was transcribed and the participants reviewed the transcript, doing some modest editing in the service of accuracy. Included in the transcript are some provocative questions and comments from members of the audience, including Dr. Ted Cantril, son of the late Dr. Hadley Cantril of Princeton University, another distinguished student of Dr. Allport.

"Gordon Allport: His Unique Contributions to Contemporary Personality and Social Psychology"

Transcription of Symposium Held at 1969 American Psychological Association Meetings in Washington, D.C.

CHAIRMAN:
Dr. Richard I. Evans
Professor of Psychology
University of Houston

PARTICIPANTS:
Dr. John Harding
Professor of Psychology
Cornell University

Dr. Thomas Pettigrew
Professor of Social Psychology
Harvard University

Dr. M. Brewster Smith
Vice-chancellor for the
    Social Sciences and
    Professor of Psychology
University of California
    (Santa Cruz)

EVANS: I felt it would be most appropriate for this symposium to bring together psychologists who actually studied with Dr. Allport. The important thing we're trying to do here is to explore how his various ideas developed and what their significance has been and continues to be to contemporary personality and social psychology. It's very interesting, I think, as you noted in my dialogue with him, how many areas he does touch on that are continually of vital interest to all of us in this field. Another thing, however, that I think is equally important and on which we all agree (this is a point that was brought up by one of our participants) is that if Dr. Allport were here, he would not be very comfortable with a eulogy. So I think that our participants are prepared to look critically at his contributions where appropriate.

By way of beginning this discussion, I'd like to simply state the kind of framework we have worked out. What we have tried to do here is to take some central ideas for which Dr. Allport has become known and we're going to call on each of the participants to share with us his perception of these ideas as related to the current scene in psychology.

Now, to say a few words about the participants. Dr. John Harding is currently in the Department of Human Development and Family Studies at Cornell University. He was a graduate student at Harvard from 1938 to 1943 when he studied with Dr. Allport, and from 1960 on he was actively working with Dr. Allport in research on prejudice. Dr. Thomas Pettigrew was a graduate student at Harvard from 1952 to 1956, and he not only did work with Dr. Allport then, but he continued on at Harvard and remained close to Dr. Allport through all the years up to his untimely death in 1967. Dr. Brewster Smith is Vice-chancellor for the Social Sciences and Professor of Psychology at the University of California (Santa Cruz). He was at Harvard first in 1941 and came back in 1945, when Dr. Allport served as a member of his dissertation committee. He continued on at Harvard as a junior faculty member and through all these years had continual contact with Dr. Allport. So, our three participants were, indeed, influenced by Dr. Allport.

To begin with, a very familiar concept of Dr. Allport's is functional autonomy of motives. It has been closely identified with him. Throughout its history it has been controversial. I might start here by asking Dr. Harding to comment on functional autonomy of motives, how he sees this train of thought, and where he thinks it's gone and where it's going. Would you like to begin?

HARDING: Well, that topic brings us right into the heart of the problem of what it was that Gordon Allport was basically trying to do. I've warned my colleagues attending the symposium that I was going to maintain perhaps a controversial thesis, and that is that there is a kind of hidden direction to a great deal of his empirical work and a great deal of his theorizing which is actually quite subversive of the enterprise which we know as "scientific psychology." I think the more one reads Gordon's basic theoretical writings, the more one is impressed with the extent to which he had a very traditional view of human dignity, and not only human dignity, but human freedom as well. I think this is perhaps one reason for his sympathy with the existential movement. And I believe that the real significance of this doctrine of functional autonomy of motives is that it asserts that people's motives are not really predictable in advance. It is, if you will, an antideterministic doctrine and I don't think he ever quite put it in that way. But I think the fact that he demonstrated example after example of ways in which motives came into being in a mature individual, which were different from what had been going on earlier, illustrates a kind of unpredictability (and he would never say complete unpredictability), but there's always a margin of freedom there. Well, that's my belief about it.

EVANS: Dr. Smith, I believe you have a comment about that.

SMITH: Well, I'd like to add a different way of looking at the same thing that John's been talking about. There is the matter of Allport's voluntarism and his concern with the unpredictability of nature. But I think the concept of functional autonomy has brought us to another major emphasis of Gordon Allport's in psychology. He was concerned with intentionality of human behavior—maybe the same thing as freedom?—the view that people are moved by positive values lying out before them in their psychological worlds and not just pushed by lacks and needs and drives. He was content to take the gospel according to John Watson or the gospel according to Freud as provisional accounts of how animals and children work, but insisted that mature adults are different. And the problem is how you get from there to here. The child might be described by lacks, by needs, by drives. The animal might be so described, but mature, adult, functioning personalities are governed by values, by intentions, by life-styles, by goals. To me, his doctrine of functional autonomy was not really a solution to this problem; it was rather a *focusing* on the problem as really a very central one for psychology. My footnote to this is that because Allport did not know children very well and did not care greatly about animals, I think he was a little uncritical in assuming for the starting point an over-simplified mechanistic view of children and animals, therefore posing the problem in a different and less promising way than we would set it up today, in the light of new data and theoretical considerations of the sort that Robert W. White reviewed in his classic paper on "competence."

EVANS: Moving to another central set of ideas in Dr. Allport's work, we find a very profound interest and very definitive work in the field of prejudice. I wonder, Dr. Pettigrew, if we could get some comments from you concerning this work in prejudice since you have been closely involved with this area of Dr. Allport's work in your own career.

PETTIGREW: During World War II Professor Allport had a stint in Washington and decided it was not for him. He returned to Cambridge and began research and writing on topics relevant to the national scene at that time. He set up studies of rumor which had not been investigated systematically. For example, he initiated a rumor seminar in 1943 which later grew into his famous prejudice seminar and is still being given at Harvard. One of his first findings about the subject was that most rumors, destructive rumors, during World War II were antigroup rumors, anti-Semitic and anti-Negro in particular; and this took him into the whole area of prejudice. He stayed at it a decade before publishing what is still, I think, the most comprehensive psychological treatment of prejudice. *The Nature of Prejudice* has now sold over a half-million copies, thanks mostly to the Doubleday Anchor paperback edition. I went to Harvard to work with him in 1952 because I heard he was working on a book about prejudice; and being Southern, I thought I knew a little something about that topic. Our difference was essentially that he had relatively less regard for sociological factors. Actually, he had helped found the Department of Sociology at Harvard in 1931, and he was one of the leading people in establishing Harvard's uniquely interdisciplinary Department of Social Relations. But he never fully accepted sociological factors as equal partners, referring to them vaguely as "distal."

But he really changed his mind on this matter, and that is the point I want to emphasize. He was the antithesis of a rigid, dogmatic theorist. I think we see it in your dialogue with him, even though he was tense and nervous in that film. He was incredibly open to experience, new data, facts; and the thing that shook him about social factors was race relations in South Africa which we visited together. He made it possible for me to go with him in 1956 for six months. It shook him not only in his conception of the nature of prejudice but in his conception of the nature of personality. There he saw men who met his definition of the mature adult, but who nevertheless were doing evil things regularly and routinely as part of their lives in an evil social system. That he began to adjust to this is evident in his book, *Pattern and Growth in Personality*. But it is even more directly evident, I think, in the preface to the Doubleday Anchor edition of *The Nature of Prejudice*, where he says in substance: "If I had to write this book over again, I would stress social-cultural factors much more than I did."

EVANS: Another central theme in Dr. Allport's work concerns his study of values. Of course, I happen to know that Dr. Brewster Smith is coming out with a book which will probably be a very fascinating examination of values in social psychology. I think it would be very interesting, Brewster, to hear some of your reactions to how you see both Gordon Allport's personal values and his studies of values because I think the two are related very closely.

SMITH: I think the topic of values is a recurring thread all the way through Gordon Allport's career of writing, dating back to when he was a visitor in Germany studying with the humanistic psychologists of the early '20s when he became acquainted with Eduard Spranger. His treatment of values represents the interesting tension between Allport as an empiricist and Allport as a philosopher. The Spranger conception of values as ideal types that give a context of meaning for the appreciation of personality goes through quite a transformation when you translate it into the Allport-Vernon-Lindzey Study of Values where, in spite of the fact that you're measuring one value against another in the framework of the single individual, what you mostly end up with in research literature is six scores that can be treated statistically.

I think the Study of Values is something of an accidental product of this tension within Allport. He nurtured it; he cared for it; he saw it revised. But the place of values in his own thinking, it seems to me, increasingly centered on his attempt to formulate a conception of the mature personality in terms of a cluster of psychologically formulated values. I think it is still debatable whether we had best conceive of them merely as values that people like Gordon Allport hold high, or rather as an intrinsically given cluster of objectively definable characteristics of the mature personality. The concept of value was central for him, and we owe much to him for keeping it before us during a period in American psychology of considerable positivism and disinterest in this realm of human meaning.

EVANS: In the dialogue, you will notice that there was quite a bit of exchange between Dr. Allport and me on the matter of expressive movements and trying to tie this into the current interest in nonverbal communication. You will note that he himself felt that his early work on expressive movements had been sort of passed by and I wonder if I can ask John Harding to comment on this whole question of Allport's studies of expressive movements.

HARDING: Well, there's no doubt that he was very
much interested in expression, style. He perhaps gave
greater weight to that than any other American personality theorist I know. I did not realize until I
observed your dialogue with him how highly he regarded his book with Vernon on the study of expressive movement. I've always admired it. The thing
which I see in that book is one of Gordon's more
successful efforts to use quantitative method for studying personality and to use it to help with delineating
a part of the structure of personality. Now he always
wanted to do that, but usually it didn't quite work
out that way, as Brewster Smith said with regard
to the Study of Values. In this book, they showed how
this paradox of apparently discrete unrelated, or almost unrelated, individual behaviors could be reconciled with some sense of consistency of the individual
through the device of "pooling," treating each bit of
behavior as if it were an item on a test and getting
more general measures of characteristics such as force
and expansiveness in a rather neat, quantitative manner. I think some of the quantitative contributions
perhaps very likely were Phillip Vernon's, as Gordon
would have been the first to say. But this satisfied
him and it illustrates, I think, again, his very steady
interest in not leaving these German notions, which
were so fascinating, about values and life-styles and
all the rest of it just at the verbal level. He wanted
to pin them down and bring them into the context
of American empirical and even behavioristic psychology.

EVANS: Another area, I think, that came through, Tom, a little bit more in the earlier parts of the dialogue than in later parts was what you yourself had observed to me was a kind of duality in Dr. Allport. I guess it is probably true that almost every American psychologist is bothered by the problem of trying to be an objective scientist, regarding psychology within a scientific, rigorous framework as against acting out his own social beliefs and commitments and trying to solve current social problems. This is, of course, one of the most important themes of this very convention, as a matter of fact. Is becoming a social actionist the proper role of the psychologist? I'm wondering how you feel Dr. Allport resolved this matter, Tom.

PETTIGREW: Well, my own biased view is that Gordon Allport would have had much to contribute to the theme of this convention. He was not only ahead of his time during his life, but still is ahead of his time. That we have not caught up with him is evident in the inadequacies we have in coping with problems presented in this convention. Objectivity and social relevance form a duality, not a conflict. I think he worked it out to his own satisfaction between, on the one hand, interest in personality, and, on the other hand, social psychology; on one hand, science and, on the other hand, social issues; on one hand, psychology and, on the other, social ethics. It ran through his days as a student. His brother Floyd had a very big influence on him in the development of the hard-nosed side which John has just mentioned.

I think he worked out in his own life many of his writings, particularly his more applied writings, by a rational synthesis of scientific psychology and relevant, effective social action. This synthesis stood out conspicuously at a time when psychology took the position essentially of what might be called "super-science," with almost complete rejection of social relevancy as a goal. It seems to me, and I am sure it would have seemed so to Gordon, that there is now a push within psychology for swinging to the other extreme and giving up scientific psychology and any specific contributions it might make in pursuit of what currently appears to be immediately relevant. Gordon would have also rejected this alternative. The message of Allport's work and his own life is that there is no necessary conflict here, that both goals can be effectively sought by a mature science.

HARDING: Well, I think I'm going to have to challenge that a little bit, really because of both sides of your thesis. I think that American psychology, at least American social psychology, had quite an activist fling before Gordon's impact was felt and I'm thinking particularly of the period of the '30s during which the Society for the Psychological Study of Social Issues, for example, was founded. Now Gordon had a part in that but before that, well, I always remember George Hartman's investigation of the effectiveness of rational and emotional propaganda appeals. He decided that the best way to investigate this, since he was running for some office on the socialist ticket, was to use his own campaign literature to test out

which approach would work. And sure enough the
emotional appeal got him more votes although it was
a difference between, I guess, two percent of the vote
in one ward and one percent of the vote in another
one. Well, you know there were other people doing
that sort of thing just in the area of prejudice. Good-
win Watson's measurement of fair-mindedness was
very actively going in the 1920s, etc. So I think that
Gordon is part of a broader movement of people who
have wanted psychology to be relevant. You mentioned John Dewey and so on.

PETTIGREW: I did not mean to imply that I think
he was necessarily the principal figure in that '30s
movement. But he kept it up in the '40s and '50s,
which from this point of view were extremely lean
years.

HARDING: Another thing is that I don't think that
he really solved the problem of how to relate facts
and values very well. And for this reason I think that
his emphasis on consistency of personality and his
desire to have a set of values which could be advo-
cated under the general heading of the values of the
mature personality led him to underemphasize the
prevalence of real, basic, value conflicts. Max Weber
is the person who I think was most tragically aware of
the irreducible clash of values which you find in yourself when you become involved in social action with
total commitment. And I don't think Gordon ever
quite faced up to that degree of commitment.

PETTIGREW: I would criticize him on the same
grounds except I remind you of the time he lectured,

I believe it was in 1945, to the Boston City Police on the subject of prejudice. He had quite a rough going over. There was, in fact, a conflict of values as it turned out and he wrote a little paper in the *Journal of Social Issues* on catharsis as a prejudice-reduction method. He faced the problem squarely again in South Africa. Of course, neither Allport nor anyone else "solved" the necessary tension between the two goals. But he recognized it, battled it throughout his life, and importantly contributed to psychology as a science and as a socially-relevant subject. Can we say as much for many members of our profession?

SMITH: He was a man of great optimism and great faith as witnessed by his expectation that he could make headway with the police in three sessions of catharsis. And as witnessed by the degree to which his faith remained unshaken by the South Africa experience. I was particularly interested in the point in your dialogue where he talks about differences that American existentialists have with the European existentialists—that the Americans don't have a sense of the tragic, the same sense of underlying chaos. Allport himself personifies this. In the areas that he touched upon in theory and in application, Allport characteristically tried to put things in a positive, optimistic way. This, of course, has it good sides, but it also has its limitations.

EVANS: One of the most recurring themes in all of Allport's work, and one that he and I certainly got into at great length in the dialogue, is his great concern with the ultimate individuality and unique-

ness of the person (idiographic approach) versus the
need for the psychologist to search for general laws
which apply to all individuals (nomothetic approach).
As you notice, I tried very hard in the dialogue to
obtain a resolution from him on this issue, but in
a sense unsuccessfully. Brewster, I'm wondering how
you feel about this. Do you think that there was an
adequate resolution of this issue in the dialogue?

SMITH: I don't think so. If we were to solve this
problem here, it would remove a fair amount of the
business of graduate seminars in personality theory.
Allport's insistence on the uniqueness of the individual is really almost more a value commitment than
it is a theoretical statement. It certainly helped to give
charter and legitimacy and respectability to the enterprise of clinicians and students of personality whose
interest was in formulating and dealing with individuals rather than in gross generalizations. But it has
always seemed to me that there is a problem here
that Allport did not fully face through: distinguish-
ing between conceptualization and artistic appreciation. The use of concepts of any sort inevitably and
intrinsically must violate uniqueness and individuality.

I think that Allport was not his own best advocate
in regard to the extent one can make productive uses
of generalizing concepts to capture pattern and organization of individuality even though some of the
uniqueness of phenomena remains neglected and un-
captured. Undoubtedly Allport would talk at this point
of how he was concerned with the developmental
laws unique to a particular individual. I think if one

pressed him hard, one would find that the moment he finds conceptual categories, the moment he uses words in the description of an individual, except in the realm of metaphor, he is giving up some aspect of individuality. Allport tried to keep the polarity of science versus art and philosophy in balance—and his commitment to science had to be at the cost of individuality.

HARDING: I'd like to comment on this. I think that Gordon's real contribution is perhaps more (I'll call it) philosophical than distinctively scientific. And by this I mean that he emphasizes this balance, as Brewster is calling it, between the generalizing urge and the nomothetic way of doing things and also the individualizing interests and the need to find the unique structure of the individual's traits. OK. This needed to be said then; it needs to be said again, as a sort of platform from which you operate. But I think he was so much concerned with saying this over and over again in various ways and in various contexts, that he didn't ever take up either of the two very, very hard tasks which remained for other people. On the nomothetic side, there's a task not just of defining common traits and finding ways of measuring them, but there's the task of trying to establish empirical generalizations, if you will, scientific laws or lawlike statements; even if you can't get complete determinism, even if you get only a reasonably high level of probability for some empirical generalization; even if it's only a correlation of .50. I don't think Gordon was ever much interested in pushing ahead with just demonstrating how strongly x was related to y, or of finding out whether or not, even in principle, y was simply dependent on x_1, x_2, x_3, x_4. That side of the scientific enterprise didn't interest him very much.

The critical idiographic side, that of working out a specific discussion and interpretation of a particular individual case, the real understanding of the individual more than just contemplating the individual, didn't interest him very much either. I think it's quite significant that his work on the individual was pretty well limited to the personal document studies. These are the studies in which the individual autobiographies contributed the data. Allport himself stayed at quite a distance. There was no attempt to push or probe or uncover. The individual is left wrapped up in a considerable mantle of mystery. And, of course, I think that if Allport were in any sense a clinician, he could not have been really content with such data. The clinician has to go beyond this. Gordon really stayed away from that.

EVANS: Many people believe Allport had a fantastic influence on contemporary psychology. As they view many of the contemporary trends in psychology, for example, the humanistic approach, the renewal of interest in religion, the tremendous research and interest in prejudice, almost everything in this vein has been attributed to Allport's influence. Does he really have this much impact?

PETTIGREW: I think in fact that he did and continues to have enormous influence on American and on international psychology, but I think now more is attributed to his influence than is in fact the case. In large part this is true because almost by definition a man ahead of his time will appear to have initiated trends which might not have come about had he not led the way. For instance, American interest in existentialism would surely have come about if Gordon Allport had never lived. But at least Gordon was responsible for it appearing a little earlier. For example, he introduced existential psychologist Victor Frankl to this country. Yet, I think it is easy to exaggerate Allport's influence. I think he had enormous influence, but a comment he made to me very late in his life is significant. With a wry smile on his face, he asked, "What does a critic do when his field comes to agree with him?"

EVANS: Although Gordon Allport said to me that he thinks of himself as being an antitrait theorist, nevertheless his classification of traits and how this in turn affected Raymond Cattell and many others is rather important in personality psychology. How do you feel about trait theories and his contribution here?

SMITH: I think that for Gordon Allport the trait concept had virtues that were as much negative as positive. He wanted a concept for the motivational and descriptive building block of personality which was not the mechanical associationistic element, not a derivative of biological drives, and which he could use in a very flexible way. Trait, as Allport conceived it, was closely akin to John Dewey's version of habit. I don't think trait as a formal concept looms as large in Allport's own thinking as it appears in the text-book renditions of it.

I would rather stress that Allport gives us an "ideal type" of theory that has the virtue of pushing one particular style of conceptualization to an extreme, while at the same time being in some ways rather unsatisfactory. That is, he has a very substantial view of personality. Even though personality is a construct, even though it is an inference, it has its roots for Allport in neurophysical dispositions. There is an imaginary sameness or concreteness to it for Allport that tended to prevent him from attending much to the interaction between personal dispositions and the situation of action as John noted earlier. I think many of us in social psychology who grew up with him found him difficult to bring along or to feel happy with because we felt he never really quite understood the modern frame of reference in social psychology that brings the psychological and sociological together rather than posing them in opposition—for which it isn't person *versus* situation, but rather person *in* situation. Lewin gave us a schematic formula for this, but it is a formula that Gordon never really was quite happy with or bought. He cared so much about personality as an existential entity that he tended to describe it and analyze it for scientific purposes in terms that don't lend themselves as well as they should to viewing these interactions.

EVANS: Tom, did you want to make any further comments?

PETTIGREW: Let me just make one quick comment.

It concerns his reluctance at receiving research grants. He did once have a large grant. It occurred in the following way. I happened to be in his office at the time a telephone call came. It was from a foundation official who said, "Gordon, we've admired your work in prejudice and would like to give you some money for your students and yourself to do more work in prejudice." This was about 1958. Gordon was dumbfounded. He put down the phone and he turned to his secretary and to me and one other person in the room, and asked, "What should I ask for?" We did not know what to say, so he screwed up his courage and in a moment, for him, of great boldness, suggested with a trembling voice, "$25,000." He meant a total of $25,000. The foundation official did not take it that way and said, "Fine. Five years, $25,000 each." Gordon put down the phone trembling and said, "I haven't got anything that an eighth of a million dollars can buy!"

SMITH: Again something that has run through several of our comments, the polarities in Gordon Allport. Remember a paper that he presented at a meeting in honor of the 100th anniversary of William James's birth. It's included in his posthumous collection, with the title, "The Productive Paradoxes of William James." As you go through that paper, you see in his dealings with James's paradoxes or polarities —in regard to mind and body, free will, positivism, the self, association, and individuality—that, point after point, these are issues that have been polarities for Gordon Allport, too. Part of the reason that we found him so interesting a person and so valuable a psychologist lies in the way in which he maintained a kind of productive tension, positions that did not fully commit him toward either end of the polarity.

DR. NOEL JENKIN (member of audience): I was present at a class in Emerson Hall the day after the historic Supreme Court decision in regard to desegregation. I remember Dr. Allport commenting upon that and saying that he was very surprised about the nature of the decision, and also that he did not believe (he was very skeptical) that it would have very much effect. He, in other words, did not believe that social change could be legislated. Now I've neither seen nor talked to him since 1955. I'm wondering if any more recent acquaintance could tell me if he changed his opinion or how he reacted to the changes that followed.

PETTIGREW: If I recall the period, his position was that he was skeptical about it actually achieving change. That is, would the law courts go along? Would in fact there be a federal and national initiative along these lines? His point was that in fact behavioral change could come first, and it usually does, prior to attitude change in the racial area. Of course, this is a very important part of his theory imbedded in *The Nature of Prejudice* volume. His whole contact theory would argue for the need for interracial schools. I remember what I think you're referring to, his skepticism about the Supreme Court decision. It wasn't that he wasn't in favor of it or that he didn't think that was in fact the direction it had to go, but he was skeptical that it would be enforced to the point where it would be achieved.

DR. TED CANTRIL (member of the audience and son of the late Hadley Cantril, another of Allport's students): I've just got two short comments. I think one of the things that accounts for the polarities that you've cited and that the panel was talking about here is Gordon Allport's attempts to account for life in real situations, not abstracted and taken into the laboratory where you can manipulate variables with a certain amount of certainty. I think this accounts for a lot of the difficulty in trying to reconcile the scientific Allport with the humanistic Allport, and I don't think it's a real polarity. I think it's a misreading. Now a very quick statement which I don't think we can develop at very great lengths. The second part is about Allport as a pedagogue. That is the importance that I attach to it in the very limited experience that I had, an experience that others shared. When one worked with Allport he would take your frame of reference and work within it. That's actually essential. Rather than starting out with essentially a negative cast, questioning premises, sort of chipping down, he would build the frame of reference and work within it, and to me this is a mark of a great teacher; which he was.

EVANS: Thank you very much, Dr. Cantril. Did any of you have a comment on Dr. Cantril's comments.

DR. STEPHEN CLARK (member of audience): I think another facet of Gordon Allport is his rather deep religious beliefs. He was actively participating with his church. As an individual, his religion may have contributed to his complexity, but he stood out at the time. I remember I was asked about psychologists who had good religious backgrounds to serve at the International Christian University in Japan. I couldn't think of very many, but Allport was one.

HARDING: Could I comment on that? Allport did have rather strong religious views. I think that they are best understood as being quite closely related to his general notions about the importance of the individual personality. His notions about freedom, which are really against determinism, I would say, and also his general social optimism illustrate this. In other words, his religious viewpoint was what theologians would call liberalism, and this has been the predominant viewpoint, I think, of American Protestantism and certainly the German Protestantism with which he came into contact in Europe. It is a viewpoint which sets great store by not rejecting the insights of science or the scientific enterprise or physiological reflexes or what have you. But there's the confidence that it can all be sort of wrapped together, and that starting with the individual, there is a sort of unfolding, a development in which man gradually finds God without the agonies or the guilt or existential anxiety or any of the sorts of things the classic theologians talked about. I think that in talking about Gordon's kind of relationship to religion, it is important to recognize that it was a special kind of religious outlook, just as his psychological outlook is a special kind of psychological outlook. There are other ways in which psychologists can relate to religion.

EVANS: Gentlemen, thank you very much. As an added dimension to the dialogue with Gordon Allport, your personal reactions stemming from your own intimate contact with him provide us with a rare glimpse into not only his contributions to contemporary personality and social psychology, but to Gordon Allport, the man.

SOME OBSERVATIONS OF THE DIALOGUE TECHNIQUE

PART VI

Overview | In this section, I present a brief analysis of the dialogue technique as used in presenting the views of outstanding contributors to psychology. Our entire series of these dialogues is placed in perspective, both historically and in terms of its potential as an added dimension in teaching.

To avoid any possible misunderstanding of the goals of this dialogue style, the inclusion of a perspective on this technique may serve to clarify our intent.

The present book constitutes the sixth[1] in a series based on dialogues with some of the world's outstanding contributors to the understanding of personality. Designed as a hopefully innovative teaching device, the series was launched in 1957 with completion of such dialogues with the late Carl Jung and Ernest Jones supported by a grant from the Fund for the Advancement of Education, and is being continued under a current grant from the National Science

[1] The other five books in the series are: R. I. Evans, *Conversations with Carl Jung and Reactions from Ernest Jones* (Princeton, N.J.: D. Van Nostrand, 1964); R. I. Evans, *Dialogue with Erich Fromm* (New York: Harper & Row, 1966); R. I. Evans, *B. F. Skinner: The Man and His Ideas* (New York: E. P. Dutton & Co., 1968); *Dialogue with Erik Erikson* (New York: Dutton Paperback, E. P. Dutton & Co., 1969); and R. I. Evans, *Psychology and Arthur Miller* (New York: E. P. Dutton & Co., 1969).

Foundation. A basic purpose of the project is to produce for teaching purposes a series of films,[2] which introduce the viewer to the interviewees' major contributions to personality psychology and to the understanding of human behavior. These films might also serve as documents of increasing value in the history of the behavioral sciences.

The volumes in this series are based on edited transcripts of the dialogues which include the text of additional audiotaped discussions as well as the content of the films. The dialogues in the print medium are intended to extend the primary goals of the films: (1) to introduce the reader to the contributor's major ideas and points of view; (2) to convey through the extemporaneousness of the dialogue style a feeling for the personality of the contributor.

Since the structure of this volume reflects an approach to teaching, some of our concerns regarding the proper communication of its intent might be shared with the reader. When we completed the Jung and Jones book (12) we thought the word "conversation" could best be used in the title to describe its process and content. However, we soon discovered that this seemed to imply to some potential readers of the book something a bit more casual and superficial than we had intended. As indicated earlier, an attempt is made to emphasize spontaneity in our interaction with our participants; this we feel adds a dimension to the project that is not usually present in more didactic forms of teaching. Yet, although these encounters are

[2] The films are distributed by Association Instructional Films, 600 Madison Avenue, New York, New York 10022.

extemporaneous, we are hopeful that this does not detract from the significance of their content. A relatively informal discussion with an outstanding contributor to a discipline, as he seriously examines his own work, should not lose significance by virtue of its informality.

A more detailed description of the philosophy and techniques of this project is reported elsewhere (13). However, a few points bearing on the content of these volumes might be emphasized here. First of all, since the questions are intended to reflect many of the published writings of the interviewee, it might be expected that a comprehensive summary of his work is evoked. However, because of the selectivity necessary in developing the questions so that the discussion can be completed within a limited time interval, it would not be fair to say the results of these sessions— either in the films, which reflect only about half the time spent with the participant, or even in the books, which reproduce the entire discussion as nearly as possible—necessarily provide the basis for an inclusive summary of the contributor's work.

Perhaps more than a comprehensive summary, we are hoping to present a model of a teaching technique which may become an additional means of compensating for the trend—observed among many of our students today—to become increasingly content with secondary sources of information concerning major contributions in various disciplines. The material resulting from our dialogues provides a novel "original source" exposure to the ideas of some leading contributors to one discipline. This in turn may stimulate the reader to go back to the original writings of the interviewee, which develop more fully the ideas presented through our "dialogue." In fact, the term "dialogue" was finally adopted instead of "conversation" to describe our content and method, since it implied, traditionally, a programmed teaching effort, in the Socratic sense. However, the interpretation of the term "dialogue" within the current academic scene often also implies a "challenge" to, if not a confrontation with, the individual being "interviewed." Furthermore, to some the term "dialogue" suggests that the questioner is simply using the individual being questioned as a tool to project his own (the questioner's) teaching role into this situation. My own goals here would preclude either of these interpretations of the term "dialogue." It is my intention that these "dialogues" comprise a constructive, novel method of teaching, and I see my interviewer role neither as the center of focus, nor as "critical challenger." I would feel that the purpose of this project has been realized if I am perceived as having merely provided a medium through which our distinguished interviewees can express their views. It might be mentioned that our interviewees have generously contributed their time to these efforts in the spirit of the teaching aims of this project. This became evident from the very beginning of the undertaking, in a letter from the late Carl Jung, reproduced in the first chapter of *Conversations with Carl Jung and Reactions from Ernest Jones* (12). Furthermore, using such sessions as a background for critical examination of the views of the participants might better be left to another

type of project, since even if this "critical set" were
to be included in my questioning, it might be difficult both to introduce the reader to the contributor's
views and to criticize them as well, within our limited
time commitment. In fact, I would expect that some
of the individuals who agreed to participate in our
project would not have done so if they had sensed
that this would become the context for a critical
attack on their work.

As a result of my experience in teaching personality
theory over the years, I have found that emphasizing
the ways in which various theorists agree or differ
with traditional Freudian theory becomes a valuable
tool for teaching. Of course, the relevance of such
an orientation is apparent in the case of some previous
subjects of the books in this series, such as Jung,
Fromm, Erikson, and Arthur Miller. Freudian theory,
even as a basis for some of the line of discussion, is
much less applicable to the subject of one of our
previous volumes, B. F. Skinner, or the subject of
this volume, Gordon W. Allport. However, this orientation is maintained at least peripherally to provide
some continuity among the several books in the series.
Another common baseline for all of the volumes is
the discussion of such theoretical trends in personality
psychology as biological, cultural, and self-determinism.

As was the case with subjects of the earlier books
in the series, it is hoped that the dialogue presentation
allows the reader to be introduced to or to re-examine
some of Allport's ideas as they are coalesced from the
particular point of view inherent in the questions

which guide the discussion. It should be pointed out, however, that in his writing, as Allport expressed himself in his own unique style, he had the opportunity to rewrite and to polish until he deemed the finished product satisfactory. In the spontaneity of our discussion, however, he was called upon to develop his ideas extemporaneously. I hope that this element of spontaneity may assist in penetrating to the "man behind the book" while losing none of the ideas central to Allport's thought. Because preservation of this naturalness of communication is essential to the purposes of each volume in this series, few liberties have been taken with the basic content of Allport's responses to my questions, although some editorial license had to be exercised to shift effectively from oral to printed communication in the service of accuracy, readability, clarity, and grammatical construction.

So this dialogue as it is presented here duplicates insofar as possible the tenor of the exchange between Dr. Allport and me as it actually took place. In spite of some of the editing which was necessary in both Allport's responses, as indicated above, and my questions, it was a pleasant surprise to review our hours of discussion content and see how few deletions and alterations were required. We hope that the flow of material, though extemporaneous, is sufficiently well organized to make this a worthwhile teaching tool. Also we hope this makes available to the reader some reactions not readily obtainable from Allport's traditional didactic presentations.

Due to Dr. Allport's untimely death, I feel that we

were fortunate in having as valuable additions to this volume Thomas Pettigrew's fine tribute to Allport in the Introduction and the symposium featuring Pettigrew, M. Brewster Smith, and John Harding, who as students of Allport had a rare opportunity to exchange impressions concerning the man and his work.

BIBLIOGRAPHY

1. Adorno, T. W., Frenkel-Brunswik, E., Levinson, D. J., and Sanford, R. N. *The Authoritarian Personality.* New York: Harper & Brothers, 1950.
2. Allport, G. W. *Personality: A Psychological Interpretation.* New York: Holt, 1937.
3. ———. *The Use of Personal Documents in Psychological Science.* New York: Social Science Research Council, Bulletin 49, 1942.
4. ———. "The Ego in Contemporary Psychology." *Psychological Review,* 1943, 50, 451–478.
5. ———. *The Individual and His Religion.* New York: Macmillan, 1950.
6. ———. *The Nature of Prejudice.* Cambridge: Addison-Wesley, 1954.
7. ———. *Becoming: Basic Considerations for a Psychology of Personality.* New Haven, Conn.: Yale University Press, 1955.
8. ———. *Pattern and Growth in Personality.* New York: Holt, Rinehart & Winston, 1961.
9. ———. *Letters from Jenny.* New York: Harcourt, Brace and World, 1965.
10. Allport, G. W., and Vernon, P. E. *Studies in Expressive Movement.* New York: Macmillan, 1933.
11. Evans, R. I. "Personal Values as Factors in Anti-Semitism." *The Journal of Abnormal and Social Psychology,* 1952, Vol. 47, 749–756.
12. ———. *Conversations with Carl Jung and Reactions from Ernest Jones.* New York: D. Van Nostrand, 1964.
13. ———. "Contributions to the History of Psychology: X. Filmed Dialogues with Notable Contributors to Psychology." *Psychological Reports,* 1969, 25. 159–164.
14. Freud, S. *The Psychopathology of Everyday Life.* New York: Macmillan, 1914.
15. Goldstein, K. *The Organism.* New York: American Book Co., 1939.
16. James, W. *Principles of Psychology.* New York: Holt, 1890.

17. Lewin, K. *A Dynamic Theory of Personality* (translated by D. K. Adams and K. E. Zener). New York: McGraw-Hill, 1935.

18. ————. *Principles of Topological Psychology* (translated by F. Heider and G. M. Heider). New York: McGraw-Hill, 1936.

19. McClelland, D. C. *Personality*. New York: William Sloane Associates, 1951.

20. Maslow, A. H. *Toward a Psychology of Being*. Princeton, New Jersey: D. Van Nostrand, 1962.

21. Osgood, C. E. "The Psychologist in International Affairs." *The American Psychologist*, 1964, Vol. 19, 114–118.

22. Rokeach, M. *The Open and Closed Mind*. New York: Basic Books, 1960.

23. Saenger, G. *The Social Psychology of Prejudice*. New York: Harper & Brothers, 1953.

24. Spranger, E. *Types of Men*. New York: Stechert, 1928.

25. Tillich, P. *The Courage To Be*. New Haven, Conn.: Yale University Press, 1952.

INDEX